JESINTEL

Jesintel

CHILDREN OF THE SETTING SUN PRODUCTIONS

WISDOM FROM COAST SALISH ELDERS

Edited by Darrell Hillaire and Natasha Frey

Photographs by Fay "Beau" Garreau Jr.

Contributions by Lynda V. Mapes and Nicole Brown

Afterword by Danita Washington

University of Washington Press Seattle

Jesintel was made possible in part by generous gifts from Jill and Joseph McKinstry and from the Hugh and Jane Ferguson Foundation.

This book was supported by the Tulalip Tribes Charitable Fund, which provides the opportunity for a sustainable and healthy community for all.

UNIVERSITY OF WASHINGTON PRESS
uwapress.uw.edu

LIBRARY OF CONGRESS CATALOGING-IN-PUBLICATION DATA

Names: Hillaire, Darrell, editor. | Frey, Natasha, editor. | Garreau, Beau, photographer. | Children of the Setting Sun Productions, issuing body.

Title: Jesintel : living wisdom from Coast Salish elders / Children of the Setting Sun Productions ; edited by Darrell Hillaire and Natasha Frey ; photographs by Fay "Beau" Garreau Jr. ; contributions by Lynda V. Mapes and Nicole Brown ; afterword by Danita Washington.

Description: Seattle : University of Washington Press, [2021]

Identifiers: LCCN 2020058448 (print) | LCCN 2020058449 (ebook) | ISBN 9780295748641 (paperback) | ISBN 9780295748658 (ebook)

Subjects: LCSH: Coast Salish Indians—Social life and customs.

Classification: LCC E99.S21 J49 2021 (print) | LCC E99.S21 (ebook) | DDC 971.1004/9794—dc23

LC record available at https://lccn.loc.gov/2020058448
LC ebook record available at https://lccn.loc.gov/2020058449

♾ This paper meets the requirements of ANSI/NISO Z39.48-1992 (Permanence of Paper).

THIS BOOK IS DEDICATED

TO THE LATE ROY EDWARDS

FROM CHEMAINUS BAY,

a beloved mentor and best friend

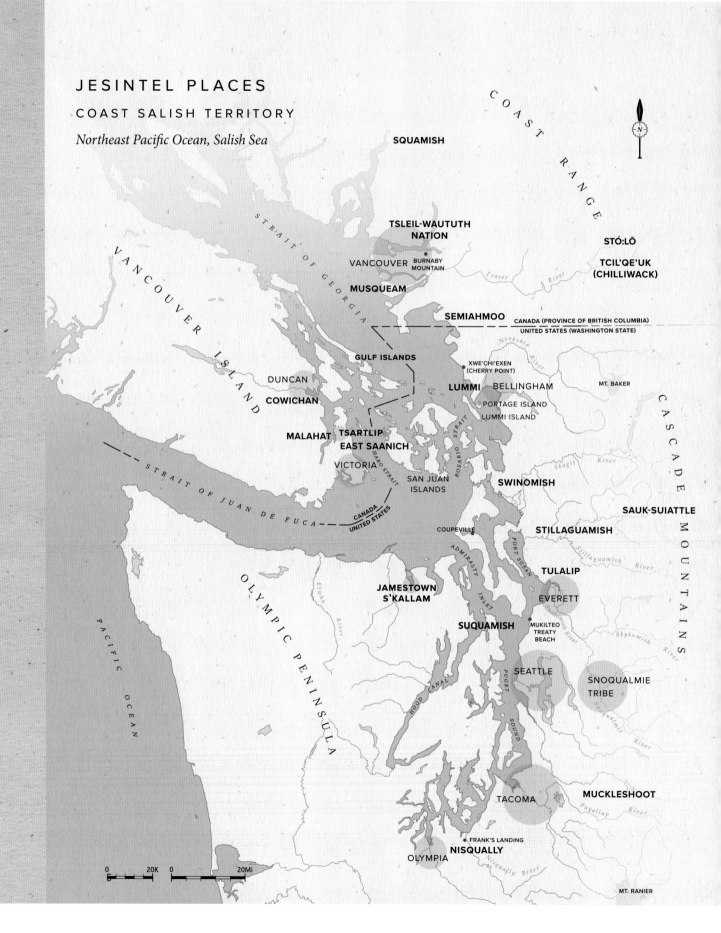

JESINTEL PLACES
COAST SALISH TERRITORY
Northeast Pacific Ocean, Salish Sea

COAST RANGE

SQUAMISH

STÓ:LŌ

TSLEIL-WAUTUTH NATION

TCIL'QE'UK (CHILLIWACK)

VANCOUVER

BURNABY MOUNTAIN

Fraser River

MUSQUEAM

STRAIT OF GEORGIA

SEMIAHMOO

CANADA (PROVINCE OF BRITISH COLUMBIA)
UNITED STATES (WASHINGTON STATE)

Nooksack River

GULF ISLANDS

XWE'CHI'EXEN (CHERRY POINT)

MT. BAKER

VANCOUVER ISLAND

DUNCAN

LUMMI   BELLINGHAM

COWICHAN

PORTAGE ISLAND
LUMMI ISLAND

MALAHAT   TSARTLIP
EAST SAANICH

VICTORIA

HARO STRAIT

Skagit River

SAN JUAN ISLANDS

ROSARIO STRAIT

SWINOMISH

CASCADE MOUNTAINS

STRAIT OF JUAN DE FUCA

CANADA
UNITED STATES

SAUK-SUIATTLE

COUPEVILLE

STILLAGUAMISH

ADMIRALTY INLET

PORT SUSAN

Stillaguamish River

TULALIP

JAMESTOWN S'KALLAM

EVERETT

Elwha River

OLYMPIC PENINSULA

SUQUAMISH

MUKILTEO TREATY BEACH

Snohomish River

Skykomish River

PACIFIC OCEAN

HOOD CANAL

SEATTLE

PUGET SOUND

SNOQUALMIE TRIBE

Snoqualmie River

TACOMA

MUCKLESHOOT

Puyallup River

FRANK'S LANDING

OLYMPIA   NISQUALLY

Nisqually River

MT. RANIER

N

0   20K   0   20Mi

CONTENTS

PREFACE

The vision for *Jesintel* comes from our respected elder Tom Sampson, who says, "We need to learn and grow together, and if we are able to do this, we will create harmony amongst the people." As the title *Jesintel*—"to learn and grow together"—indicates, there is more than one community at the heart of this work. Like the seasonal round and harvest, Coast Salish culture is dynamic and diverse, yet bound together by shared values and relations. Such connection creates and generates a resilient culture and worldview, and it is not just humans involved in this creation and generation. Within all things, there is an interconnectedness with places, land, water, and the spirit that recognizes ethical reciprocal relationships.

So, then, the people, places, and expressions of culture that hold this work together are interconnected—practically and in spirit—like the traditional village sites that landscape the territories and patterns of Coast Salish culture since time immemorial.

Gathering and sharing stories is a Coast Salish lifeway, our She'lang'en. "This is our way of life," we say—the breath and the song, the wind and the paddle, the fire to the salmon, the cedar tree's shade, the cedar basket and cedar hat, and the tectonic shifts of the earth, the drum, and the dance. It is the understanding that animals, plants, material objects, rivers, mountains, forests, and essentially all aspects of the world, and the whole universe, (be)come together through story and the values of gathering and sharing.

This coming together builds a vision and a responsibility to listen and to share, straight from the heart. Relations are at the heart of this work and inform how this gathering has been brought together through a complex yet natural understanding of place and time. Long-standing relations helped build this volume of cultural sharing and trust. Dear reader, the gathering and coming together of friends and relatives for this work have happened through the practice of honoring natural laws and protocols and the boundless relations of Coast Salish people and their territory.

The University of Washington Press asked how we chose the people and places to be included in this work and this book. Essentially, how were we clear and specific without elevating ourselves or any individual part? Well, we were having a gathering, and we invited witnesses from each part of our homeland. These are the ones who agreed to have us to their homes and places of worship, to visit with their families and gifts, to share time together at casinos, cultural centers, and all around Coast Salish territory.

Together, we knew the work that was to be done and recognized, and who the people and the places to do this work were. *Jesintel* is a gathering of stories about our futures and living stories about our past, place, and people—a way to provide for, respect, and cultivate the health and resiliency of the generations who came before and those who will come after.

As you attend this gathering, we ask you to listen carefully to a call to recognize a way of remembering our teachings of abundance, suffering, resilience, connection, and ultimately joy.

As the old people have taught, each of us carries gifts to learn together and to share with future generations. Such ancestral teachings on the pursuit of spirit convey the essence of natural law and the power of the giveaway in Coast Salish culture.

The ancestors' wisdom is carried by the elders and their relationships with the land, and the water, and the people, plants, and animals—the shared and common homeland. Through their understandings and teachings, the old people are in touch with our past and the relationships that the past has with our present and future. This reciprocal commitment among all things—past, present, and future—upholds our sacred obligation to respect the teachings and the gifts of our elders, conveying the essence of Coast Salish values.

As Coast Salish people, our territory and relations are intersected by an international border between superpowers, yet stories told by the elders demonstrate the continued existence of Coast Salish jurisdictional community. Natural law exists outside of linear and colonial understandings of time and space, taking place instead through intergenerational stories and relations.

The living stories curated to these pages are highly specific to Coast Salish culture, family relations, and accustomed places. Yet at the same time, they are related to building an outward-facing global understanding of relationships and responsibilities toward intergenerational learning and cultural heritage revitalization. Though the conversations and interviews that cultivated the words and images in this book took place within a span of several years, the teachings they uphold are timeless.

If we reflect on this gathering of people and what is being shared in this way and at this time, important threads become visible and are made stronger from the Salish Sea, across Indian Country, and among Indigenous peoples worldwide. Weaving understandings of how our traditional values inform education, environmental stewardship, family, and sovereignty throughout broader society aligns with the greatest attainment of inherent rights.

By sharing our cultural teachings, *Jesintel* communicates some of the transformational power of our traditions through a combination of personal narrative, photography, and elements of design.

Because we are a people whose ancestors, belongings, and territory have been taken, exhibited, fragmented, and occupied through the process of colonial settlement, the publishing of *Jesintel* underscores the importance of maintaining relations and traditions despite historical interference.

We must remember and teach, not only for ourselves but also for the broader society, our brothers and sisters who wish to learn and grow together.

We invite broad exchange with this work. Most important, we invite tribal youth, members, and leaders. We also invite public audiences who wish to know more about the Coast Salish lifeway and our living culture through remembering and storytelling. Focusing on the importance of learning, we ask teachers and educators to weave this work into their curricula. We also invite regional, statewide, and national leaders who wish to grow their understanding of connection and shared sacred responsibility.

This work brings the past forward and bears witness to highly specific and varied remembrances shared through oral traditions, songs, dance, story, anecdotes, and family and place names. These are not stories of singularity but are rather living and emerging stories that come from our infinite and timeless connections and relationships. The result is a dynamic glimpse of a culture alive, one that values cultural identity—that we may learn and grow together.

Jesintel.

ACKNOWLEDGMENTS

My dear people, on behalf of Children of the Setting Sun Productions, our Board, staff, and family—we are grateful for this book as a gift to the people. Our hands go up in thanks to the many people who made this work happen.

Our journey would not have been possible without the support of so many kindhearted people. From the beginning, CSSP has been supported in its work by three individual, anonymous donors. We thank these donors for sharing in our vision and for providing the resources needed to begin the project. In addition to our three original donors, the *Jesintel* publishing project was funded by NOVO Foundation, the Potlatch Fund, the Satterberg Foundation, Group Health Foundation, and the Stillaguamish, Puyallup, Squaxin, Port Gamble S'Klallam, Lummi, and Chehalis tribal community contribution funds. Hysh'qe to all those who have supported the publication process.

As a new production company we have come to know many Salish elders who have been the strength and guiding light of their respective communities. The creator has blessed us with the rich gift of friendship, making this work possible. We raise our hands in thanks to all of the elders who participated in this work, and to their families. This project would not have existed were it not for the rich knowledge and ability to retell, to remember, so cherished and demonstrated by our elders. The many gifts we received in carrying out this work are incomparable. It has been a humbling experience for the CSSP team to learn of the elders' gifts and to witness the manner in which they carry these.

From concept to fruition, our co-creative progression has been very much embodied by the name *Jesintel*—"to learn and grow together"—as pronounced by Elder Tom Sampson when asked what to call the project and publication. We wish to thank Tom for his inspiring and formative gift in naming this work.

In addition to our elders, the project has benefited from advisors and contributors Danita Washington and Ron Tso, Lynda Mapes, Nicole Brown, PhD, designer Tara Almond of Taradactyl Design, and the team at the University of Washington

Press, especially Larin McLaughlin, Ellen Wheatley, Jennifer Comeau, and Mellon University Press fellows Hanni Jalil and Jason Alley. We wish to thank them for their support, guidance, and advice throughout this process.

Thanks go to Lynda Mapes for connecting us with UW Press, reviewing our work, and writing the gemlike essays that accompany each chapter narrative, providing context and background for the reader.

We must acknowledge, this project has depended on the shared vision of our core project team: photographer Beau Garreau, DAKO5. Studios, and project editor Natasha Frey. Beau captured the photographic image of every elder, making moments of visual impact real throughout each interview, and Natasha led the co-creative process, guiding our extended team of contributors from creative vision to manuscript completion.

A heartfelt thank-you to Sabeqwa de los Angeles and Shamania James for their assistance with transcribing interview audio files, Santana Rabang for her assistance in administrating the editorial process, and Elli Smith for her review and edits. Hysh'qe to Tara, Sabeqwa, Shamania, Santana, and Elli; their steady presence at various stages of manuscript completion has moved this process along and is greatly appreciated.

And finally, we hold in highest regard our dear friends and relatives Danita Washington and Ron Tso. Thank you for being a touchstone of spiritual guidance and advice, bringing much-needed words, songs, and prayers to this process.

We could not have done this without all of your gifts.

CHILDREN OF THE SETTING SUN PRODUCTIONS (CSSP) is a Native-owned and -operated 501(c)(3) organization located in Bellingham, Washington, within five miles of the Lummi Nation. CSSP descends from Great-Grandfather Frank Hillaire, who despite the outlawing of Native spirituality, song, dance, and ceremony, formed the Children of the Setting Sun Song and Dance Group for the purpose of continuing and sharing the culture of the Lummi Nation. The traditional Lummi song and dance group included several of his grandchildren. Prior to his passing, Frank instructed his grandchildren to "keep my fires burning." We endeavor to follow his instructions as an organization and with this publication.

Since 2012 Darrell Hillaire, a great-grandson of Frank Hillaire and CSSP's executive director, has led the projects based upon his lifetime relationships with the many elders, leaders, and youths within the Coast Salish territory. As a new production company we have come to know many Salish elders who have been the strength and guiding light of their respective communities. The creator has blessed us with the rich gift of friendship, making this work possible.

JESINTEL

TOM SAMPSON

TSARTLIP FIRST NATION

I've lived my life on the shores of Saanich Inlet, Vancouver Island. Our tradition is that the firstborn always goes to the grandparents. So, I was the oldest of twelve children, raised by my great-grandmother—the lady who taught me everything and raised my father before me. Her English name was Lucy Sampson, and she was of the Hileox Halalt. She was a remarkable woman. We did not know her exact age, but the baptism records said she was over 120 years [old] when she died about thirty years ago. I came to live with her when I was two years old, and she was in her eighties. She taught me history, my place in the world, spiritual beliefs, and all about the natural world, in both of our languages—*HELKEMINEM* from Cowichan and *SENĆOŦEN* from Saanich.

We want to grow together. Yeah, the *Jesintel*—it's knowing what you're going to grow into. Here I am. That's me. You know what I mean? I think once you say who you are, you grow. The creation story teaches this too.

"This is who we are."

What that really does is open the door. And you've got all these other things after you walk in. Once the Creator said, "Okay, you're here now, this is who you are, now here are your relatives." Then you begin to work on understanding each one of them.

THE IMPORTANCE OF NATIVE LANGUAGE

The urgent work of teaching and recovering Native languages is underway across Coast Salish territory.

Many Indigenous nations have created their own schools where their Native language is being taught at the earliest grades. For some tribes and bands, elders have patiently recorded their people's first dictionaries.

This work is helping heal the legacy of a bitter history of forced assimilation, especially with respect to white-run Indian boarding schools, where children were punished for speaking their languages.

Language is at the core of culture. In homes, at gatherings, and in ceremony, Coast Salish languages are being spoken again. With each word, wholeness is being recovered. —LYNDA V. MAPES

OUR CREATION STORY

My dear friends and relatives, I want to thank you for being here.

I'm going to talk to you about a time when there was only what they call the first part of creation. The human beings were the last to be created. My father carved this story pole to tell our story.

The human being is always at the bottom of the order of beings because he was the last to be created.

Us humans, we were asked to watch and to observe everything that was around us, and our great-great-grandparents pointed to the water. "Look at the ocean, look at the water, your brother is out there. His name is K̲ELOLEMEĆEN. He is called the killer whale."

It is not true, he is not a killer whale. He is the spirit of our ancestors, and the spirit he has is the one that we carry. He has a song. You children have to remember the songs of these people who come from the ocean, whether it is the killer whale, or the sea lion, or the many citizens that live in the ocean, that have a story to tell us human beings.

So my father began to talk about this, because my father learned this from his grandmother, grandfathers, and all those people before him.

The other one he went to was called the eagle. The story of the eagle tells about a time when this bird flew in the sky, and saw everything that needs to be seen, and took care of the people. And this bird, the eagle, has a song. You hear his song. You will hear him, and there is a message for our people that there is another world to be looked at. And so this eagle has his own song also.

We come to the [living] land that we walk on. Many times as we walk on this earth we see different things, but this one is special to our people. In the English language they call him the serpent; in our language we call him TSI NEŁKI. He's a spirit, and he has a voice.

He has a song that belongs to our children, that belongs to our family. Every one of us humans has this gift, but our people—the people of the Coast Salish—carry those songs to this day. So we tell these stories to our children to remind them of our relationship to one another, of the land, the sky, and the water.

Then we come to the wolf. The wolf is our oldest teacher of what a family is about. It is not only the wolf; it is the cougar or mountain lion, the W̱TEKNEĆ. These two, as well as the bear, the SPÁET, they have a spirit. Many times throughout the winter, we see these spirits dance in our home.

These are things we learned to have a relationship with, not only with our human people, but also the spirit of the first part of creation. At the time of creation these were all human beings, because they were here before us. We had to learn how to live with each one of these spirits, because if we didn't learn we would become poor in our own way. So they sang the songs that belong to each one of these spirits and each one of these brothers. We call them ŚWOLEK̲E (many brothers), and ŚWOK̲E (one brother): these are our brothers.

Whether they're in the ocean, the land, the sky, or the rivers, these are the things we have to protect. Our grandparents said to us, "Remember, remember, this is who we are. This is who we will always be. Never, never let your children forget who they are. This is who we are."

Tom Sampson shares Creation Story and staff during the production of the play *What About Those Promises?* (2013).

2

LANGUAGE AND COMMUNICATION

The elders always told us never to forget to identify yourself: "This is who I am." They always talked that way in the big house. I was seven when I went to school and learned to speak English. I was totally brought up in *SENĆOŦEN* from Saanich and *HELḴEMINEM* from Cowichan. I didn't know nothing else, so when I went to school I had one heck of a time trying to adjust to the English language, because without my own language, who was I?

At Saanich, Cowichan, Chemainus, *PENÁLEXET*, Musqueam, and Squamish, when you talk to people, it's not about a community no more. It's about the way that family talks. Like, we have a word, an example that we use now, *Ā,LEṈ*, your "home" [he pronounces *Ā,LEṈ* three ways]. It's all the same word, but said differently in different families because of their accent, the way they talk.

So, when you're speaking in the longhouse, and these people get up and talk, you don't have to ask who they are. You can tell, by their accent and the sounds they make, where they're from. But educators try to make us all sound alike. And what happens then is the family loses its family accent. It's critically important to keep the family accents, because they tell us what family and region each person is from.

When teachers make the sound of the letter and the alphabet (international alphabet), it takes away the natural sound of who we are. And that's what language is all about. You see an eagle or a raven and you know exactly what they're going to sound like. They never change their natural sound.

So, I got a great-grandson. When going fishing, and we're coming home, and my younger son, he has a small fish about this size. He said, "Okay, Junior, sing the eagle song." So, my uncle grabs a piece of wood, and he goes like this [he starts beating on the table]. And my grandson starts to sound like an eagle. Pretty soon, the eagles come out of the tree and then he throws the fish out to them.

You see, the sound is a form of communication. It tells where you're from. And, whether you're a raven or an eagle, you know. A seagull is even different—*Ḵ,ENI*. They actually say who they are—*Ḵ,ENI*. That's our word for seagull. So, when the eagle talks, that's the way he says it: "*Kwani, kwani, kwani!*" He's actually saying who he is, because that's the sound they make.

See, we don't know how to do things like that anymore. We've become very structured to English and French. I don't speak French. I used to, by the way. I spoke both French and Latin when I was going to high school. But English, I

Tom with Coast and Straits Salish Declaration Drum. The signed drum declares inherent rights to the lands, water, and resources.

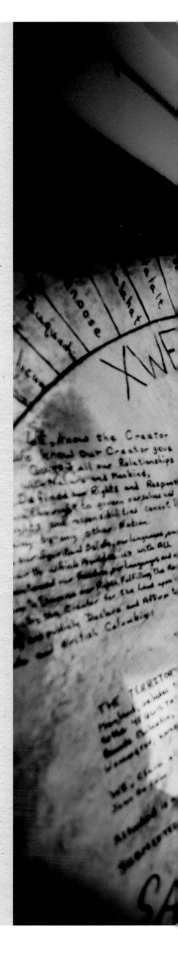

Tom has shared the Creation Story throughout the Coast and Straits Salish region.

Tom at home, laughing.

couldn't do it. I failed every test I took in English. I couldn't spell "again," you know, a-g-a-i-n? I kept spelling it a-g-n or a-g-i-n. I couldn't spell it right. So, I think that's what's wrong with our education system.

Teachers are trying to tell you that you're saying something wrong, and they are doing it in our schools, especially in the immersion program. There's no family sound, just a linguist sound. Because of the way the letters are written, you know, it exactly sounds this way. And so that's not helping us. It's compromising not only the language but also the family. We're literally pushing the family out of the way, through this use of the language.

Well, you know, that's what one of the elders said a long time ago. He said, "When you're talking, the words you use gotta look like a picture." You know? So that word stays with you. You know, it's easy to say, "You're beautiful." That's the quick way to say it, but if I really want to paint that picture about your beauty, I gotta say it in a way that describes your beauty, so you can remember it.

The language is very explicit about how we treat sound because you're painting the picture at the same time. You're showing what the person looks like or what a thing looks like. Everything, even our songs are like that. From the creation story we learn the killer whale has a voice. In the wintertime, a lot of our people sound like a killer whale, their voice. A lot of our men and women sound like a mountain lion. They make that sound.

You see, these things, it's the natural way of doing things. We are not trying to make it, perfect it. We don't have to design something. We don't gotta program it! How do you program an eagle to change his voice? Or the wolf to change his sound and his habit? It just doesn't happen.

We're trying hard. But society is trying hard to destroy that process—the natural process. See, we're just like all things, like the creation story I carry and share. When I tell that creation story, wherever and whenever, all the story does is open the door. Here's what you got to know now. Here's the wolf. Here's the serpent. Here's the things that were here long before you, before us. And they know what to say. And they know what to do.

So, that story then—that creation story we did—when doing it with the carving,

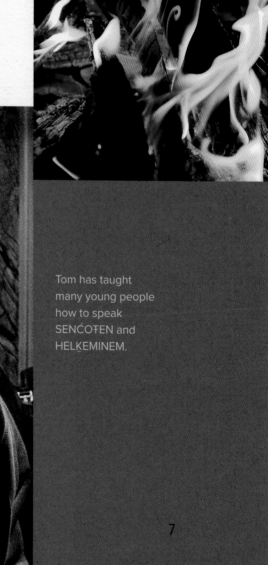

Fire is an important element of spirituality for Tom and many First Nations peoples.

Tom has taught many young people how to speak SENĆOŦEN and HELKEMINEM.

7

opposite
Tom frequently presents in educational settings and in convenings where policy and law concerning First Nations are being considered.

it was actually just opening the door to where we need to go. A lot of people phone me from all over the place to ask me how I learned that.

And I say, "Well, every winter, we gather in our longhouse. And we talk in our language. And we sing the songs that are thousands and thousands of years old. And we have a process for doing that. So when we watch our women dancing, we see them making particular gestures and steps. They're showing us, 'This is who I am. This is my spirit.' And the women do that and the men, too."

Now we have to begin to define for ourselves what Indigenous means to us. So, when you look in the dictionary, get some ideas about what the dictionary says. You know, it's in our language. "Indigenous" is called *TUO*—"at the very beginning," *NIŁ TUO*, "they were here first." See, we have to be able to say that, but we also got to be able to explain it. It's good to say, "Hey, I'm an Indigenous person." But if you can't tell them what "Nation," what "Tribe" this Indigenous person is, it doesn't mean a heck of a lot to the government.

We need to really work hard with that right now. Last summer, I was at a conference on the justice system. Lawyers, and judges, and prosecutors, and this man called Finch. He's a Supreme Court judge in British Columbia. He said, "We have a duty. An ultimate duty to learn about these people's law now." It's called common law. And out of common law, there comes this word in the language, TUO. "At the very beginning," that's what it means.

Our language is about survival. If we don't know how to say something properly, then we'll die. And my grandfather was the one who showed me that, and my grandmother, and I tell this story all the time.

IT'S NOT LIKE THAT TODAY

You know, I went to court many times over my lifetime on hunting rights. Until they asked me one day—the Supreme Court of Canada, the lawyer Louise Mandell—she said, "Can you describe night hunting with a light?" And I said, "Yeah, 'cause that's how my grandparents do it. For hunting deer, ducks, crabs, everything that was in the ocean, they used the light." But what light was that?

My grandfather took me to the forest, and this stump was rotten. It was rotten and the bark was peeling off. He said, "Okay, go to the middle of the stump, the dead tree." So, I peel everything back. The center of a rotten stump is like the orange. So, when you light it on fire, it's brighter than this. It's called *ĆEMEX*. And then you gotta find a way to hold the light, and that's called *ḴÍWEĆ*—"the prop that holds it in place." Together, this is the *ĆEḴÁN*, "the torch."

So, when we went to the Supreme Court Justice of Canada, and I explained that to them, they said, "These people have a right to hunt at nighttime. They've

When I was about ten years old, you know the canoes out there—out in the bay where I live—they were all fishing. And I watched the people pulling in fish. So I went home and I told my mom and my dad, "I want a canoe."

"Oh, go talk to Great-Grandma."

So I said to Great-Grandma, "Can I get a canoe?"

And she said, "Why do you want a canoe?"

"I wanna go fishing."

"Why do you want to go fishing?"

"Well, everybody's out there."

My grandmother and my grandfather took me down to the beach. "Here, you want a canoe?"

I said, "Yeah, I want it real badly. I need it."

So my grandfather brought the canoe to the shore. It was about the length from me to you. "Get on." So I got on. Sat there.

"Now what?"

"Go a bit farther out. Okay, tip yourself over."

And I said, "Why?"

"Tip yourself over! You said you wanted a canoe! The first thing you gotta learn is what this canoe's about."

So I paddled out and finally, I tipped the canoe over, and I came up out of the water. It must have been ten or twelve feet deep. And I was scrambling on top of the canoe.

And my grandfather says, "What are you trying to do?"

"I want to get on top of the canoe because it's cold!"

"Ohhhh, my, boy, you're a really poor child. Go under the canoe."

So I went under the canoe. Son of a gun! There's a lot of space here. There's this much air space under the canoe [he motions with his hands]. Because the canoes were made out of cedar, and cedar doesn't sink, so as soon as it tips over, it rises up like that.

So if you're way out in the ocean, and nobody can help you, that's where you gotta go, underneath the canoe. See, it's a way of survival. You gotta know the water, you gotta know the canoe.

My grandfather asked me, "Which is the worst wind?" I said, "Oh, the north wind. It's cold." "No. It's not the north wind. It's the west wind, 'cause it comes down real hard and fast," where I live.

So everything then—this relationship with survival—comes from our language, comes from experience. Everything I learned comes from my grandparents, my uncles, and my dad. They were all fishermen and hunters, everything.

been doing it forever." And that's how we won our case, because the language is considered by the Court as holding the evidence of our having hunted at night for centuries. Again, it was the language that done it.

So, all these things that come out of our traditional languages are connected. *TEKLÁLEN*: our languages contain all we need to know about transferring of wealth such as ceremonies, lands, names, access to resources, and so on. There's so many illustrations, demonstrations, of how the land and waters are connected together, in terms of the environment being part of our language and lifeways. There is just no way of measuring it or even saying, "I know, I know now." I don't. I don't know everything. But I do know what I learned from my grandparents and my great-grandma.

But, if we're gonna need to keep declaring sovereignty and Indigenous rights, we better know our language. It doesn't mean anything if we don't know it. I've said this many times to the colleges and universities and some of our teachers.

OUR BIRTHRIGHT, SCHELANGEN

The old people—like Isadore Tom—soon as they saw us, they came to embrace us. And they said, "How can I help you?" See, we don't know how to do that anymore. When those old people died, that went with them.

We now have to have certificates, social workers, economic development officers, citizenship registration: blood quantum defining "membership"—one-quarter, one-third, one-half, 5 percent, that's what we have to do now, to our own people. So, we've kept the apartheid system alive here, by doing that.

You have to know your birthright, and that's called Schelangen. Where I'm from, Schelangen is "the way I live." Your Schelangen means your culture, your language, your history—everything—it comes down to one word. You don't have to say all those words because they're built in. You know, your ceremonies, whatever they are, it's all in that one word. *ĆELÁES* is "inside the birthright," within our way of life. It's called *SYEWÁN* in *HELḴEMINEM*.

You see, all of this is in our language. It goes back to that sound, that sound of the language. A lot of tribes today are struggling with that, because they're trying to compromise their language to fit into another language, and once you start compromising your language, trying to make it fit into another language, we're in deep trouble. It's gotta stay the same as it has always been.

It just don't fit. You know, I've been asked many times, "Why do you guys say sacred water?" I say, "Ask my wife, ask my mother." 'Cause I was born in water. And I stayed there until my mother released me: *XÁXE SŁÁNI*. We say *XÁXE ḴO*, "the sacred water," because it comes from a woman.

The older women were very frank about the way life is, the way it should be. We learned what the stages are, the seven stages of change for a woman. A man goes through only six stages in life. We're one short because we don't know how to have babies, and that's how the women taught it.

That's why we look at where the salmon go. Salmon are no different from humans. They find the cleanest water to put their eggs down in, and then the male puts the sperm on top of the eggs, and it's gotta be clean water. No different from a human being. It's the language that says that, you know? "We're just like a salmon." Yeah, but I don't look like a fishhead, you know? [he laughs].

VIRGINIA CROSS

MUCKLESHOOT TRIBE

We've had men also, but I think the women have generally dominated the Tribal Council seats. Marie Starr, Charlotte Williams, and I have been on the council. Well, I've been on since about 1980, almost forty years. It's been kind of traditional for the Muckleshoot to have women leaders.

When I was still in high school, Annie Garrison was our chairwoman, and she was also the judge at that time. She carried a heavy stick. And what she said went; nobody questioned her decisions. Whatever Annie said, you agreed to.

I remember my mom, Alvina King George, and dad, George J. Cross Sr., hadn't been married, and a fellow came down and said, "Annie says that you've been here long enough and you have all these kids and you have to get married." So they said, "Oh, okay." So my mom and dad got married and made us legal.

When I was young we got involved with working for the tribe. I was the first Head Start Services director for the tribe, and our program is now fifty-one years old. At that time we had a woman tribal leader, Bertha McJoe, who, along with her family and cultural roles, had been on the council for a number of years. Before that, Bernice White was chairperson, and before that, Annie Garrison was chair.

THE INDIAN BOARDING SCHOOLS

Tribal councils across Coast Salish territory are taking great pride in and investing heavily in education for their people from the earliest grades. Record numbers of Indian and First Nation students are earning diplomas from high schools, colleges, and graduate schools and mastering specialized training, from medicine to law and all sorts of trades.

Many tribes and bands have started their own schools, and tribal governments also are providing scholarships to send students of all ages throughout the country and the world to the school, college, or university of their choice.

The Native education renaissance underway across Coast Salish territory is a triumph over the past, when beginning in the 1880s Indian children were sent by the federal governments of the United States and Canada to compulsory, white-run boarding schools. Those boarding schools operated in the US through the 1920s and in Canada until 1996. The schools were intended to forcibly erase Native identity, language, and culture. Healing and recovery from that violence is ongoing. —LVM

When I was first working for the tribe, we developed a preschool program, and then we applied for federal dollars and it turned into a Head Start program. At that time the tribe had no money or resources. Our leader, Bertha McJoe, was very committed to the tribe.

I would go to meetings with her. At that time she was buying her own gas for her car. She bought her own lunch. She was so diligent about taking care of tribal affairs, and she paid for it with her own money. And she had no money. She later on became our Indian language teacher for the tribal school district until she passed away.

Perspectives on the Boldt Decision. Contemporary ledger art by Robert Upham.

"WE CAME FROM A LARGE FAMILY"

Bertha McJoe was a beautiful lady. She was also Levi Hamilton's mother. He was tribal chairman for a short time, and he passed away in a fishing accident.

We had no tribal office to keep our records in. She kept two or three boxes under her bed and that was where we kept the tribal enrollment. That was our archives department, under her bed. I would go to see her because I became the Head Start director, and she would haul the materials out from under her bed, and we would go through them. That was how we started.

I think you sacrifice your kids, your own family, because you are committed to the tribe. My kids were supported by my family and husband at that time. I divorced him later, but when the kids were small, he was home with the kids. And I always had a sister or friend who would come in and help with the kids when I was at work. Even when we would have to go to the hospital or on urgent trips, one of my sisters would come and watch my kids for me. They were real supportive.

My dad was a Puyallup. So, I'm Puyallup and Muckleshoot. My grandma and grandfather on my mother's side were Muckleshoot. On my father's side, they were both Puyallup. Grandma used to say, "Oh well, we're Cowlitz, we're Yakama." And she would name off all kinds of tribes.

Our dad let us choose our tribe, I remember, when I was about nine or ten years old. They wanted us to enroll in a tribe, and so he asked us what we wanted to be. And we told him Muckleshoot. I'm sure it hurt his feelings, because he wanted us to be Puyallup, but we lived here. It was home.

I think we still stick together as a family somewhat, but I don't think it's as tight as it used to be. I think we were a lot closer when I was younger. We didn't have anything else. We grew up with no electricity and no water. You know, like everybody did at that time.

Our grandma, Mary King George Charles, was my mother's mother, and she was "everybody's grandma." She traveled quite a bit, and she would take us with her. She would visit people, sometimes to visit the Shaker Church, sometimes for celebrations. At that time there were no phones or internet, so if you wanted to see somebody, you had to go see them. She would take different grandchildren with her, and so we got to travel to different reservations, even with no money.

I am most proud of what we've done in education. The tribal council is committed to education, our favorite cause.

We have the birth-to-three preschool program, and then we have the Head Start program, then we've got the K–12 tribal school, then we have a nonaccredited college for now. Every year we contribute funding to educational departments,

Virginia says she has witnessed her community grow and strengthen through education.

15

Cedar is valued in daily use and ceremonial purposes: the roots, the bark, wood, and withes.

center
Coast Salish weavers used three basic basketry techniques: coiling, twining, and plaiting.

homeless organizations, classroom Indian education, and sometimes veterans' organizations. We try to give as much as we can to the schools. Most of our money came in from bingo and the casino. We finally had enough funds to provide the tribe with a variety of services—housing, health, education. I pressed a lot for elder services. We put a lot of money into our scholarship program. It's paying off now. We probably approve about a hundred scholarships per year. When we first started the scholarship program, there were only four of us with college degrees. Now we have over a hundred who have degrees.

TANANAMOUS FOREST

We bought a forest about eight years ago. With the forest, we have ninety-six thousand acres of land that is within our traditional territory along highway 410. It goes through Mount Rainier to Enumclaw and up the road on either side of the highway, to Chinook Pass. People ask us what we're going to develop on that. We're not developing anything. We're just going to keep it. We're going to keep it for the tribal members who want to go fishing, hunting, and gathering. The White River runs through it, and there are trees, deer, and elk. We get a lot of cedar out of the forest for making baskets and things. We have one day per year called Tananamous Day for all tribal members to go up there. We have a forest crew up there of kids—young people. They spend a lot more time there. There's about twenty of them, young men and young women. They're up there making trails, providing a road for Tananamous Day, they do a variety of things. My granddaughter's up there working with them, and they love it. It's done so much for them. We just want to keep it.

One of the fish that the tribe invested in, even before we had the land, is the springer salmon (Chinook), because we had won a case with Puget Sound Power and Light on the White River in 1978 or so. Since we didn't have any money in 1978/1979 to pay the attorney fees, the Native American Rights Fund (NARF) won that case for us. One of the conditions was to restore the springer salmon in the White River, and that has finally paid off. I had notice just recently that one of the first springers has come back up the river. So the springer salmon was a major fish product for our tribe, and we just love it. There are also trout and other kinds of salmon in the river now. We hunt for deer and elk, and once in a while we do drawings for goats and sheep, the rams—no more than five per year for the goats and rams.

A lot of gathering goes on throughout the year. In the spring and early summer we gather cedar. We have one tribal member, Val Seagrest, who got her degree in native plants and nutrition, and she has really pushed all of us to try to use natural medicines and remedies rather than some of the medicines from the clinic. I called her a few weeks ago because my sister has cirrhosis of the liver, and she recommended nettle tea for kidney and liver problems. She provides us with elderberry syrup and just about anything she can gather naturally.

The land is sacred because that's where our families traveled—our ancestors traveled in those woods. The trails, and the berries, and the hunting, they did all of that before we were here.

We named it Tananamous: Land of Power.

Right now, it's about land. We're trying to buy as much land back as we can get. I think some of the non-tribal public are threatened by it a little bit. Right now we're trying to put Emerald Downs racecourse into a trust. That's going to take the property off the tax rolls, so we'll have to negotiate with the city of Auburn. We're doing pretty well with our water rights. We had a lawsuit against the power company back in the early 1980s that resolved the water rights on the White River,

Virginia's office walls include photos of family members, state leaders, and former presidents.

Virginia is most proud that the Muckleshoot people have come "from nothing" and overcome "struggle and uncertainty."

which comes down from Mount Rainier. With the help of the Native American Rights Fund, we won that fight.

It has taken years, but now we have over a hundred people with college degrees. It's a big jump from when we started out in the 1970s.

I went to the University of Puget Sound and then got a master's degree in education at the University of Washington in curriculum and instruction. I started the Virginia Cross Program when I was with the Auburn School District in the 1980s, and it has grown. It's now known as the Virginia Cross Native American Education Center. When I started the program, we had a lot of kids who had dropped out of school, and we designed the program to serve the cultural, social, and academic needs of teenagers who weren't in school. The program now supports students from over seventy tribes across a range of areas that are all connected. It's important for our tribal students and future leaders to learn and share their culture as part of their education. It's important to share this with non-tribal students and neighboring community members.

opposite Virginia holds a family photo.

19

I have a lot of hope for the new legislation requiring Washington State public schools to offer a Native Education curriculum. We helped. Our lobbyists worked really hard on that. When it was signed, we went to the signing ceremony. If the public schools follow through and teach what they're supposed to be teaching—the history of how tribal sovereignty came to be, treaty rights, Native science, opportunities to learn our traditional languages, opportunities to participate in traditional practices—then I think that our kids will have an easier time than we did at school. I worked for the Auburn School District for over twenty years, so I know very well the kinds of history books they approve and are distributed into our school system. Nothing has to do with tribal history or the plants you might gather. They don't mention anything about Muckleshoot tribe or hardly any Indian tribe. They don't recognize that we have our own constitution and bylaws—they only study the US Constitution. They also celebrated holidays that we don't honor—Columbus Day, now Indigenous Peoples' Day. I don't think they have treated our kids well for their special needs.

I'm thinking back to when I was in school. I graduated in 1957, and at that time I was the only Muckleshoot graduate. My sister two years before me was the only Muckleshoot graduate. We would start in kindergarten with ten or fifteen tribal people, and by the time we were out of the eighth or ninth grade, they would all be gone. It just didn't serve our kids or our people well.

I think there was just so much prejudice. There were very few of us who were in high school at that time, probably not more than ten of us in the whole school of thousands of kids. Our dad wanted us to be in school, that's why we were there.

I think it's the education department that has really progressed, mostly because that's where our primary interest has been. We now have a tribal school and a Lushootseed language program with a program director, where we teach and qualify five full-time language teachers every year, who then go out to teach. And now we have hired another five more. Hopefully we'll end up with everybody speaking Lushootseed language. And hopefully this work will continue.

And we have very good elders' programs. That's an emphasis I've received from my elder women mentors. When our people turn fifty-five, they are eligible to have a home built, and they are eligible for a small monthly income, handicap assistance, and chore service.

We try to take care of our elders. We don't give much of a guaranteed income, or per capita payments, here. That's probably a contention here on the reservation. We give three per capita payments to tribal members a year, and they're small. We provide services rather than per capitas.

We have daycare. We have childcare. We have the education programs, schol-

arships, and all those kinds of things. And we have a resource center for families in need. All of our members can have however many years they want to attend college with expenses paid. We've had three people earn doctorates in the past five years, and they're all women.

The men—well, there are not many fish out there. They're not making a living at it anymore. They would love to fish and would spend their life fishing if they could. They now just do it for fun.

The biggest challenge for the Muckleshoot tribe has been retaining our sovereignty. Most tribes that I know have had to wait out previous presidential administrations—even to realize our voting rights. A lot of our cases that we've had to file against the United States have been decided in our favor. There are cleanups that need to happen in our rivers, and most of us would like to gain back our traditional lands. There is so much work to still be done. We're trying to retain our sovereignty and get along with the non-Indian communities around us. We haven't paid as much attention to that as we should.

ERNESTINE GENSAW

LUMMI NATION

The more you work with things, the more you are close to the earth, and the more you touch things on earth, the more you know what to do with them.

These ancient objects [she points to items] were found at Portage Island. They are a mortar and pestle for grinding. Artifacts are still found on the beach there, when you're beachcombing. This is an anchor. See what the Indians did. They knew how to make sinkers for fishing. These are prehistoric. I don't even know how old they are.

KEEPING YOUR HANDS BUSY

Gathering, preparing, and sharing traditional foods from the land and sea in locations used for thousands of years is a central cultural practice and way of life in Coast Salish families. Fishermen speak of hearing their ancestors talk when they are out on the water. These deep ties to the land, the sea, the medicinal plants and berries and roots, fish, and game, have sustained the people in a way no other foods can. These are first foods.

"Keep your hands busy," said the late Lummi elder and weaver Fran James (Ernestine's sister), who liked to celebrate her birthdays on the beach with friends and relatives. Her birthday treat was freshly dug clams, steamed on the beach in the traditional manner in sand pits with seaweed or barbecued on yew sticks by the fire.

Knowledge of the rivers, the sea, the plants, and animals through all their seasons, and hereditary rights passed down through generations, guided the harvest. Digging spring's first roots and gathering summer berries. Carefully stripping fresh cedar bark and preparing and weaving it. Carving the cedar tree's soft yet water-resistant wood. Ceremonially cleansing the spirit, body, and home with fragrant cedar boughs. Participating in these practices is part of what it means to be Coast Salish.

Knowledge of these skills and arts is beyond words. It's knowing where to be when—to gather, to hunt, to fish, to weave, to carve—and needing to do these things because that is what your people always did. And so, the traditions continue. —LVM

Ernestine recalls stories of her childhood on Portage Island.

I must've been four or five by the time we first moved over to Portage Island, off the end of Lummi Peninsula. I was born here at Lummi in Marietta, and we lived down at Fish Point and Red River. My dad had property on Red River. And from there, we lived in shacks.

The kids don't know what a shack is, so I have to tell them, "It's a shack, with boards up, with holes in it." You know, you could see the sun shining through our house. When I'd wake up, I'd see the sunbeams coming through.

Portage Island was a place for me to be. I felt free, and it was a good environment for me. The air was good. We lived off the sea, and our food was mostly seafood. Portage Island was a place where Grandma Lizzy Mulberg had a house up on the hill, and my aunt Alice had a house on the other side of our place. It was property owned by Grandma, and we inherited land from Grandma Lizzy to us families. It was beautiful. The weather was so nice. In the winter, we did have snow over there, but not like the winters today. My dad was a logger and fisherman, and Uncle Art also lived over there. I'd say Grandma was the boss on Portage Island.

We had fruit trees. We had a lot of fruit trees. We had sheep. We had cows and horses. And, this time of year, it would be haying time. They'd cut the hay. The menfolk from the mainland would come across, and they would volunteer their time haying—cutting, shocking, and hauling the hay into the barn for Grandma to feed her cows in the wintertime.

Ernestine loves sharing her garden and knowledge of traditional plants.

Also, later in the summer Grandma would get the crew of men to herd and shear sheep. We herded the sheep clear around Portage Island. They would mark the sheep once they were in the corral, and the men would cut the wool off with shears. They would mark the ears. Everyone had a differently marked ear: "This is my sheep, that's your sheep."

Grandma was very tough. I thought Grandma was a mean lady, but all the time she was teaching me how to work. And my cousin Violet Hillaire and I, we had to make lemonade. Grandma made us do that, 'cause we had to get the water from the well. She had a good water well there.

We knew we had to work. We knew we had to go and do our duty—all work and no play. If we did play, after we finished our work, we got to swim all day in the water, in the salt water. So, after our work was finished, my cousins and I would go swimming, stay in the water till dark.

At Portage Island we lived and crossed over to the Lummi Peninsula in a rowboat every day—a rowboat to come to Lummi Day School. So Uncle Art's children would come across on his boat, and my dad would cross on our boat, every day, regardless of the weather (because the weather was really windy over there sometimes). And we learned how to row a boat, my cousin Violet and I. It was a lot of fun. I thought I owned the whole Portage Island! That was when I was young. I had to help my grandma row a boat around Lummi Island when I was nine years old.

We didn't have an outboard, so we rowed to go trolling for salmon. We ate lots of seafood—sea urchin, clams, horse clams, crabs—hardly any beef. We had to eat mutton. I didn't like mutton. And we ate the fish that is under the rocks called a grunter, sqwa'. I didn't learn too much of my Lummi language because every time the old ladies would be sitting in the living room talking in the Lummi language, they would stop talking because they did not want us to learn the language, because it wasn't allowed.

We no longer live on Portage Island, but there are fishing and canoeing camps seasonally, and our people walk and row out to the island regularly. [Portage Island has gone back to Tribal title and management through conservation measures.]

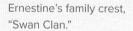

Ernestine's family crest, "Swan Clan."

Ernestine's family surrounds her.

BOARDING SCHOOL

I went to a boarding school in Salem, Oregon, when I was twelve. That was after my dad passed. He drowned at Portage Island in our little rowboat. So, my mom and my brother and sister, we moved off the island, and I went to the boarding school for six years—Chemawa Indian School in Salem, Oregon—and I graduated in 1949 from there.

There, I didn't eat very much because there was like a thousand kids there—Indians from all over the Northwest and different places. It was the second year, maybe, that I got acquainted with girls and boys from different tribes. I was only

above Ernestine collects angels and swans.

right A chart of Ernestine's children's and grandchildren's birthdays. Ernestine says, "I've enjoyed watching my children and grandchildren. I don't even know how many I have but I know I have quite a few."

twelve when I went, and I knew I was Indian then. After I mingled with other Indians, I knew, okay, there are different kinds of Indians besides me. I thought I owned Portage Island? Of course that's not true.

There was prejudice among other tribes. There was prejudice within Indian Country, for a lot of reasons. I can't explain it—how I felt. It was an academic and vocational school. So I learned how to sew. I learned how to cook. I learned how to can foods. I learned that from my grandmother also, but I learned it more in the boarding school.

My grandma made us can and learn other ways to prepare and preserve foods when I was very young, but when I went to the boarding school, we learned vocational training. Vocational training was girl things, boy things. For the boys, they farmed, they did electrical work, carpenter work. And for the girls, it was work at home.

SWAN CLAN

We belong to the Swan Clan. My grannie, that's the other side of my family. Grandpa Balch, he lived in the woods. He saw two swans—a male and a female, se'litse and so'litse. They told him what their names were. Because Indians talk to birds, animals, they told him, "I'm Se'litse, and I'm So'litse." That was a boy and a girl. Grandpa Balch had a song, and my sister, Beverly Cagey, sings the song. So, we belong to the Swan Clan. That's on my mom's side.

I get lonesome for Portage, for the water. Water is my life, sea life. Even if it took my dad . . . This is our way of life—the water, the sea, salt water. In fact, I have a grandson that's in Alaska. His first time up there, and he's learning how to fish up there. Also, I married a fisherman, construction worker, canoe puller [strong paddler]. I had nine children. I have eight now. I lost one of my daughters.

All my children went to school. I made sure they went to high school, finished their high school. Because I thought it was really important that they all have a good education. My oldest daughter has gone to school forever—college, college, college, forever. She's doing well. All my kids are okay, as far as I know, you know? And, my Tim. Tim, my grandson, is the chairman of the Lummi Nation. When he comes to visit, he doesn't talk politics or anything. He doesn't talk about any problems. He just comes and visits. He takes care of his family really well. A couple of my girls have been teacher's aides for the Lummi School. My one son was a policeman for the Lummi police, and the other ones are canoe pullers.

STEVEN AND GWEN POINT

STÓ:LŌ NATION

STEVEN POINT I'm Steven Point—that's my given name in English, for the government at school, of course. I was given the traditional name Xwaliqxweltel. I guess I must have been seventeen or eighteen years old when my mum gave me that name.

My mum is Rena Point. She used to be a Boland before she got married to my dad, Burley Point. My dad was from Musqueam, British Columbia. He was raised around the other Points there, but the Points originate in Kilgard, near Sumas. My dad's father was Abraham Point, and his father was Charlie Point.

NATIVE FAMILY VALUES

The importance of family can't be overstated in Native life. When Coast Salish people introduce themselves, it is with not only their own name but the names of the people they are descended from.

The extended family has an important role in child-rearing. Grandparents, aunts, and uncles are key caregivers for young children in their first years of life. This frees up parents to do the work of supporting the family. It also broadens the task of teaching and learning to a wider community and brings in a rich range of knowledge and skills.

The idea of obedience is both practical and spiritual. Spirit is a guiding force in day-to-day life, not a special occasion of worship on a holiday, or Sunday.

Obedience is not only to elders and to community teachings but to spirit—that is, to the understanding that each of us has a purpose in this life and that we must finish that which we are here to do. We are all different, and each person has something to offer the community. We must accept and obey that calling; the community relies on each person to do his or her part.

Balance too is a Native family value. Present in nature, so too must balance be present in families, governments, and within each of us—our male and female sides, our strengths and weaknesses, our good and bad impulses. Balance is a universal law: staying in control, staying in a state of awareness, not being fearful or blocked or angry. Harmony is closely tended and cared for, through disciplined behavior. Nasty words are believed to come back as illnesses and accidents. People can become sick because of bad behavior.

These are Native family values in spirit-guided lives. —LVM

Charlie was the first to come to Kilgard, and he was first cousins with old Frank Hillaire, who was also from Kilgard.

My mom's mother was Ann Silver. She was from Kilgard. My parents were actually related. Their marriage was arranged, one of the last marriages arranged by the elders. My mum tells the story. She was sixteen years old. My dad was eighteen. Amelia Hillaire, from Lummi, came to the meeting. She was mom's aunt. She represented Lummi at that meeting.

My elders are from up in Chilliwack and Musqueam. Because my mother is the granddaughter of the hereditary chief up in Kilgard, she became the carrier, which is the person who holds the Schelangen, which is our right to self-govern. So, that's where I come from.

You belong to your mother in our culture. My mother is the head of the wolf clan. The wolf clan comes from Kilgard. That's where my name comes from.

One hundred years ago, there wasn't any US-Canada border. People moved back and forth pretty freely, up until the government put the border in. Now, my dad's living in Skowkale, where we were raised as kids.

So that's who I am: Xwaliqxweltel. I'm a speaker of the house for the wolf clan. That's what my name means. My mother is the matriarch of the Stillagway. She's the holder of the sqwi-gwi—"human face mask"—from her ancestors, where the mask came out of the ground and out of the water. So, we carry [have responsibility for] that now, my family. We still carry that.

My mother is still alive. She's our boss. We were seeing if women have power. In the old days, it was the men that did the speaking. They fought in the wars. They fed the people. But the actual running of the affairs, that was done by the women, because they owned everything. They owned the property. The property is different from what white people think of as property. Names, songs, stories, all of that belonged to the culture, belonged to the women. In those days, when you got married you had to move to your wife's house and live with her [he laughs]. My uncle used to talk about that. Children belong with their mother.

GWEN POINT Uts'ith-ga-itsa. [She begins speaking in her Native language.] I thank you. Tsit'tholetsel. I thank you for—we say "siyoyes"—the good work that you are doing.

My name is Gwen Point. We've been married for forty-five years, come April.

Tselwiyuk is the traditional name for the region where we live, and the more contemporary name for the reserves is Skowkale. Tselwiyuk is surrounded by reserves. They're all small reserves, and we probably live on the smallest reserve.

My family line is Shoysqwelwhet. If you know my name, you would connect me to my father's father's grandmother. And just from what Steven said, you would also know that I am displaced.

My mother was Irene, and she married Oliver Peters. Today, there's a reserve called Peters Reserve. This was where the big family was based, the extended family—the Peters family's secret island in the Peters Reserve.

But my mother, when she was very young, all the children were put in residential school. My mother's mother, Matilda, died giving birth. Her grandmother, who was Celestine, was still alive, and would have taken the young children, the traditional way. But the government wouldn't let the children be raised by Celestine. They just took them all to residential school.

I later found out that my mother's mother, Matilda, was also sent to residential school. So two generations were raised in residential school. And it was a harsh time for our family and our communities. And my mother, as a result of the boarding school's teaching, wouldn't speak the Native language nor have anything to do with our traditions.

Steven and Gwen listen, and laugh, together.

So, she married my father, who was from Sts'ailes. Sts'ailes means "a beating heart." If you go there, you'll see the water going over the rocks, and it looks like a heart beating, so Sts'ailes.

My father was Don Felix. And his parents were Felix Joe and Dolly Felix—we called her Sophie as well.

My grandfather's connection would be back to Tselwiyuk. He told me that when he was young, he would be taken to the head of the lake on the other side of Harrison Lake by his grandmother, at the beginning of the summer. Then, at the end of the summer, she would take him back to Tselwiyuk.

My name comes from my grandfather's, my father's father's, grandmother. And my grandfather claimed us, even though you're supposed to come through your mother's line for names. Because of my mother's family's two generations in residential school, a lot of them had no way to claim their own names, or were afraid to do so, and a lot of our names were lost.

When we joined our ceremonies, I was a young girl. And my grandfather stood up and covered me with his grandmother's name. My name means "one who helps people." Shoysqwelwhet, "one who works for her people." That's pretty much who I am.

Gwen introduces herself by sharing her family relations and home.

KNOW YOUR FAMILY LINE

Gwen speaks
of going home.

GWEN Oh yes, Leonard Peters is connected to Sts'ailes, directly connected. But we're related to them through my father's father. Yeah, the Peters.

It's confusing—the Peters. What they would do in residential school is they'd say, "Okay, all of you are Peters and all of you are Joe." That's how the staff named our people in the schools, because they couldn't say the traditional names. So they would say, "Okay, your name is Mary, your name is Bill. You're on this side, your last names are Peters," to try to keep track of everybody. So it's confusing because my mother's family are Peters, but earlier some of them were named Joe.

My mother's mother married a man named Joe Hall, and there were the two brothers that came up from the States, and we now had a connection to Tulalip.

STEVE Now, I worked in some of the residential schools, and my dad went to Sechelt there. Bobby Joseph was telling us a story. You know how schools today, they will do intramural sports? So, they call one class the Bears, one class the Cougars, and so they have a name for their class, right?

35

Well, they did that in residential school, but they used the names of the saints. So, "This is the Joseph class. This is the St. Peter class. This is the St. John class." So when our young people would go home, their families would ask, "What is the name the school is calling you?" "Oh, Peter, I only got one name."

Just has one name, so when he has a son and others would ask, "What are you going to call him?" he would say, "I want his name to be Peter too." "Oh, okay, but you need a last name." So they would take the name of their father as first and last names. So it's Peter Peters, John Johns, William Williams. See, there's lots of that in our territory because of the residential schools. This is how we came to have these European names as surnames.

And sometimes people would be working on a farm, and they'd need a number, like a Social Insurance Number. So they need to apply for one, and they don't have an English name. So my dad's grandfather worked for the Wells. He would crack open the Bible and choose the first name he saw: "Oh, your name is Dan." Then he'd crack it again, and it would fall on Milo. And that's how my dad got his full name, Dan Milo.

GWEN My grandfather, their legal Indian last name was Joe. His father's name was Felix Joe, legally. But my grandfather didn't like the last name Joe, so he took his father's first name and called himself Richard Felix. So some of our family members are Felix and some of our family members are Joe. And I went by Gwen Felix because I thought that was my last name, until I had to go get my driver's license. They said, "That's not your last name."

That's why they said, "You are who your mother is." You have to be able to say who your mother's-mother's-mother's mother is to say who you truly are.

STEVE In the old days, you couldn't marry your cousin because they knew that the children wouldn't come out right. There's a place up there called Telahi, where deformed children were left. They knew, from experience, the problems of marrying close.

So the reason they had the meetings, first of all, was to see how closely they were related. The other reason was the whole territory. Like, if this table was our territory, they'd say, "You know, the last marriage we had with Lummi is gone. A person died. We need somebody to marry Lummi."

"Oh, how come?"

"Well, you know, we still get our clams there" [points at a spot on the table]. Or, "They supported us in the last war we had, you know? We owe them that." Or, "Oh no, we got somebody lined up over there [points at another spot]. We

Gwen shares stories of resilience with a sense of humor.

need somebody up here [points at another spot] because they talk politics now." This was the protocol around connections. They have to make the connections to these different places to keep the peace. And it was a way of keeping our nation together. So the elders would want to make sure that when they come in the door, "They say that's our family." "Why?" "Because we married, see?"

It was like United States sitting down with England saying, "Okay, we have these ties." They do that in Europe. They used to marry people back and forth to cement ties. And that's exactly what these meetings were about. It was to form a relationship. Sometimes you needed access to certain fishing sites. If you were related directly, of course, there was a pecking order. They got first dibs on that fishing site.

Now, if you're married, you get second dibs on that fishing site, you see? Then you get to set your net after they got all their fish. So access to resources was certainly a consideration. Hooligan and cranberries were down at New Westminster. Well, the big fields were there. We needed to make sure we had access to that [he laughs]. So this was the politics behind these meetings.

GWEN And that was one of the last things my grandmother said to me before—you know, because she didn't have the money to go off all the time. So when we did go, she would tell me all these things, who the people are, and she said, "And don't forget, we have cranberry fields in New West." And I thought, cranberries? Okay, so guess what they grow down there? In that whole area—you know it's a multimillion-dollar production—cranberries. Yeah, and I want to tell those people, "I think those are our cranberries." They have no idea. She said, "That mountain, this is where you go to get your cedar."

THEY WERE TOLD

STEVE Nasty words come back to you and they become illnesses. You get sick from what you say.

But we tell people to be proud of who they are. That first becomes important because when they went to school, they were told that they were savages, that they were heathens, that they worshipped the devil. They were told that they were wrong, that they shouldn't speak their language, that they were going to die in hell—all these things they were told.

So all of our people who went to these schools came back with inferiority complexes. They believed that they were less than. This connects with a lot of our work today with younger generations—when I began working in the schools, trying to encourage young people to try to make them feel good about who they were, to try to make them feel better about being brown. To have brown hair,

coming from a reservation, right? Because those that looked more Native got discriminated against more than those who didn't.

It was hard for them to survive that, so we try to tell them to feel proud of who they are. But I know that some of the families look back, and maybe they do this with their nose [he sticks his nose up in the air], right? Which we're not supposed to do, even the nobles didn't do that. They didn't look down on other people, even for the captives; it was against our culture to do that. But humans are humans.

People who want to find their way up the social ladder will claim that they are from these places that they're not. Just because they don't want the stigma. But all these things—so many things changed when the smallpox happened, when the Europeans came.

The biggest change that came was in our ethos, our philosophy, which didn't get to be transferred from one person to the next because 90 percent of the people died. So many of the elders were gone.

Steve laughs with editor Darrell Hillaire.

The reason we reach back now to understand how the culture worked before is for the issue of self-government. We had our own government. The government ran the nation. It ran the people. There were laws that they abided by, and there was order. And to suggest that Indigenous peoples in the New World lacked structure is wrong. To suggest that they lacked spirituality and religion is wrong. To suggest that they were heathens and uncivilized is wrong.

So much has changed. But we look back to those days to bring back some of the roots of our own government—our identity—so that we have something to give to our next generations. We can leave some of the baggage behind, so maybe we should.

GWEN Many years ago, I was asked, "How do you choose?" [between traditional knowledge and a higher education]. And I said, "You don't." What you're doing here is a good example of how to bring those two together.

When I was going to university, it was not easy. Going to high school was not

Steve shares love
and laughter.

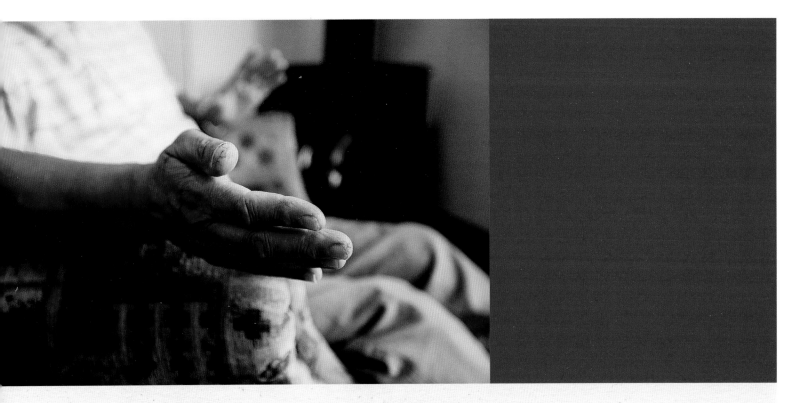

easy. I went to a First Nations' band–controlled school. I was a straight-A student. It was a result, though, of having an ear condition. My ears weren't good, and I suffered from earaches. So I stayed indoors, and I couldn't swim, so I would just start reading.

And I read anything and everything because we didn't have books in our homes. I think it's really important to remember that we come from an oral tradition, not a written tradition. We didn't grow up with a writing system; all of that is being created with our language today.

Education for our families has not been a good experience.

NOW WE'RE CONNECTED

GWEN And for many it's still not. So that's why doing something like this book project is so important. Because—I see it in not very many communities, but you'll see it in our families—we're basically nonverbal. Think about that: we have an oral tradition, but we're nonverbal, for the reason that Steven mentioned.

What you say goes out and comes back. In our tradition, my grandmother told me, "You have two ears and one mouth. You keep these open, and this quiet." But the way she would say it, it was so kind. That's who your teachers were in our families, your grandparents—it wasn't your parents, it was your grandparents.

Understanding that is huge. You're nonverbal—we didn't grow up in a classroom setting with words. Rather, in our traditions, your first teacher was your grandmother. Everything I understand I've learned from her, my father's mother.

And I think that for me, it was also a result of being confined and not being able to play. Everybody would be outside or be swimming, so I spent a lot of time inside, and I was with my grandmother most of the time. And she said the first three years of a child's life are the most crucial. That forms their character. So it was the grandparents that raised the children in those first three years. And that freed up the parents to do the work.

When I was a young parent, it was different by then—this tradition had changed. Now there's nobody to watch the children. Well, back in the day, the grandparents did. It wasn't the parents, when they were getting older, that taught the children. It was the aunts and uncles, for good reason.

Because you just think about the parent-child relationship. If you tell your child, "Fix your bed. Take out the garbage," they kind of groan, right? And they'll drag their feet. Sometimes you have to tell them two or three times. But if an aunt or uncle tells them, they're more willing. And that's the same for a parent. If I make a basket with my niece, she can do no wrong. But if I make a basket with my daughter, all I can see are her mistakes. So we had a way of learning and teaching in our communities. But over here, in this nontraditional setting, you're given words. And I learned all of this from being a teacher and being an assistant. It could be French or written German. We had no connection to those words.

Our people—the ones who are traditional (and a lot of them are), the ones not raised with the written word—are figural learners and symbolic learners. And making that leap to that type of learning is a struggle.

And the other is being nonverbal. I remember growing up, and if my uncle walked in the room, I walked out. If elders walked into the room, you got up and walked, and let them sit down. We stood, we didn't sit. And I see that in my community today, but nobody's telling you that. Nobody's telling you, "Get up, and move for the elder person." Nobody's telling you to be nonverbal. That's just a way of life.

When I was in university, I'd have to force myself to look at somebody. Every time I did, it felt like I got hit. It would hurt. Even now it hurts. Because it so went against everything I was raised with, and even my children were raised a little different.

I remember sitting at a dinner table, and Steven was in university, and my kids were talking and talking. After a while I felt like there's something wrong here, and I just started crying and went upstairs. My daughter came up and she goes, "Mom, what's the matter?"—thinking I'm lonesome or something, because

Steven was at university in Vancouver. And I said, "I don't know, but I think you kids talk too much."

Because it was so against our tradition. So you've got all of this happening, and you're throwing it in a basket, and there's confusion, right? So when I was going to university, I had to work really, really hard, and one of the biggest things I had to do was make that transition. But I didn't understand what it was. It was a real challenge.

When it came time to go to UBC [the University of British Columbia], I was afraid. I was always afraid. I now know what that is inside here—it's fear. And I know that's what a lot of our young people live with, is this fear. I phoned my grandmother, who was still alive. And she always knew when something was wrong, and she said, "What's wrong?" And I said, "I gotta go to UBC, the university. I don't think I can do it." And she said, "Well, why not?" And I said, "I don't know. I don't think I can handle the racism and discrimination. I just don't think I can handle it." Because it's everywhere, it's every day, it's all the time.

And back then it was a bit more open. You know, people would just look at you and say, "You're not welcome here." I know that look. I know what racism looks like. I know what discrimination looks like. And I know what it feels like. And that's the fear that's there.

And I was really hoping my grandmother would say something.

But she was quiet. For a long time, I thought the line got lost, she hung up on me or something. And she said, "You go. Just don't forget who you are." And I thought, How am I going to forget who I am? [she laughs]. At the same time, I didn't know what she meant. How do you forget who you are?

So education is a challenge. And what helped me was hearing that history—that early history, learning about the residential school, understanding that history, helped me appreciate where I am. It's hard to feel sorry for yourself when you find out what your parents went through, about the laws that were imposed. It's harder to feel sorry for yourself when you find out what your grandparents went through, and your great-grandparents.

Then you think about this strength that they had. The strength that they had to walk through what they had to walk through, and still . . .

OUR GRANDMOTHERS

GWEN My grandmother was just this amazing person who shared story after story after story.

And if you can imagine, we were at the ceremony yesterday. We were with

Gwen carries hope
and healing to her people.

our children, and grandchildren, and grand-nephews and -nieces. And what's important to understand is what we tell the young people today, "You take care of this. You take care of what we have, because of our history." And our young people need to know that history.

Every American, every Canadian in North America needs to know this history. The tragic errors, but if you flip it around it's, wow, the strength that came from the resolve of those people that carried that. Because our ceremonies today were only stories when we were young.

And young people say to me, "What should I do? You know, is this right?" And I tell them, "When I was growing up, I could do everything backward, but in my grandmother's eyes I could do no wrong. But she said, 'You check this, and you check this, before you use this.'" And one of the things that is so important is that you're not afraid when they haul you on the carpet.

I've been hauled on the carpet in front of the elders many times, and our leaders. And they'd say, "What are you doing? Why are you doing this?" But if you can explain your intention, and that it's good, they'll go, "Okay."

I've been hauled in front of the elders because they did not want our language in the public system, and I wanted it in all of the schools. And they hauled me in front and said, "We don't want our language in the public schools. We don't want white people speaking our language when it was ripped out of us. I don't want a white person speaking the language. I was beaten for that. I didn't even teach it to my children. Why do you want to do this?"

And I actually didn't have an answer. But I looked at them, and I said, "Well, I think, in my mind our language shouldn't be a second language. It should be the first language. And everybody in Stó:lō territory should be speaking HELḰEMI-NEM. Because in our language are our values of kindness and respect. There are words in our language that have so much meaning. Can you imagine if everyone spoke HELḰEMINEM what a good place we would live in?"

And they sat there and said, "Okay, you can do it."

So how do you balance? You just do. I don't choose. So many things have been said to us over the years, even by our own people. "How can you be an Indian?" "You can't go back to your ways. You can't go back to your way of living."

And my grandmother said, "We're not afraid of change." She said her grandmother was the first one to trade her basket for an iron pot. And we grew up with stories of the Ice Age and the flood, because our people weren't afraid of change. [Gwen introduces herself in the language.] No matter where I am, whether I'm in my regalia, or sitting in a longhouse, or in downtown Vancouver speaking at a conference, I'm still the same.

SPIRIT AND BALANCE

STEVE On top of that, Gwen has the Sqwedilech Board and gets called to hospitals in the middle of the night. We both are called to hospitals to pray for people. Any time of the day people come to our house for help. Sometimes it's three in the morning, and we have to get up and cook for them, help them. She's been called to Alberta; she's been called to a lot of different places.

In our culture she has to go, so I go with her.

Right now I'm building a longhouse. I'm the chairman of that committee, to build the longhouse. It's another project that I'm doing, you know?

Like Gwen, I also do spiritual work in our communities. I don't know if we think about balance that much. Balancing? We just take the kids wherever we go. They come with us. They come with us when we go to do spiritual work. They run for us. I have poles, she has the boards, and they've had to come with us wherever we go.

But what I understand is that in your journey, the journey that you're on, you're given choices. You make up your mind, what you're gonna do, and you do it. And because you've made up your mind, because this is something that is put on your path to do, the spirit looks after you and looks after your family, so that you can do this—what you're told to do, what you have to do, right? You're supposed to go do that, then. And that means making sacrifices. It means loss of time with your family, but you came to this world to do that. That's your purpose. You have a purpose in this life. You can't stop doing it. You have to finish that which you do. It's been assigned to you, what you've accepted.

And balance is a rule of the universe. It's just a rule—a law—it exists out there. We can't do nothing about that, it's just a law. If things get too much this way, it swings back the other way. People think that the president of the United States is a bad person, and that maybe he's not going to do well. Well, we'll swing back the other way eventually. It's the rule of balance. It's just the way it goes.

People come to me and they say, "Gee, my life is really out of whack." And I say, "Is it your life, or is it you?"

Really, balance begins with you, it's within you, right? If you're a balanced person—in other words, you're walking on the trail that you've got and you're doing the best you can and you're not being critical of others, you're helping them out—you're living your purpose. You're balanced in your life.

But if you feel like your life is crazy, it's a whirlwind, "I don't know what I'm doing," kind of disorganized, then I'll stop you and say, "Well, let's talk about you." You know, "What's happening with you?"

Because the rule of balance is a universal rule, but it's also in you as a person. We have these two sides—the male side and the female side—and you have choices to do good or not to do good. You can be helpful or not helpful. You can share or you can be stingy. But whatever you choose, it affects this balance. So if you don't give, eventually something will happen that will force you to give—you can lose everything. It's just balance, it's the universal law.

GWEN Do what you're supposed to be doing. A canoe for me is really, really special. And it was the last thing my dad did for me. I was ten, eleven years old,

and he'd been sick. All the years I remember, my dad was sick. I understand they were hunting in the winter, and he got lost. My grandmother told me this story when I was older. He had been trying to find his way back and connect with everybody else. He fell in this bit of a hole, sort of, and he couldn't get out. He tried a number of times to get out of this hole, and the snow was high.

But the last thing he did, before he died, he took me up to the river. The river that we call Chehalis, at Sts'ailes. And we went down to the river, just the two of us. He said, "Come on, come with me." And I said, "Okay." We got in the car, went down to the river, and he goes, "You go down there, and you listen to those people." I said, "Okay."

Nobody said, This is what you do, this is how you do it—just, Get in there, in the canoe. And then they started canoeing. So my arms got tired. He said, "Just keep time." Have you ever been in a canoe? My arms were tired. You're going upriver, right? So I was tired. But there started my canoeing.

And I was lucky to race with a lot of the older women. And back then we had

Steven and Gwen support each other's service.

47

Ed Leon. He was an elder in the community. He'd come over, and the elders are so kind, and there you are with your real skinny, little arms, and he's feeling your arms. Measuring your arms. He said, "Good, you'll be good on the bow. Long arms." He liked my long arms.

So before I left, over the years, they put me on the bow. Back then the canoes were bigger on the front, or not really small. Because I physically would have to go on one knee to turn the canoe. But the canoes today, just [she makes a whoosh sound], they're able to turn the canoe on the bow.

But now my granddaughter's eight, going to be nine. So I told her the other day, that she has to get on the canoe now, because that's when her mum started. She was nine years old, go for a ride, right? [she laughs].

STEVE I think about the times when you're low on strength, on . . . "conviction" might be a better word, that's when doubt begins to cloud your mind. You start doubting yourself. You start doubting things that you're doing. Sometimes doubt comes from your friends, sometimes it comes from people you're working with, sometimes it's just inbred into yourself. Doubt is a blockage. Conviction is the strength that you need to accomplish that which you want to do.

Fear is another one. Being afraid—afraid of heights, afraid of people, afraid of crowds, just being afraid. It's a barrier that stops your conviction to achieve that which you want to get done. Some people stop early, they give up, they quit. They can't go on, they feel too heavy, too tired. They feel like they've lost their faith, they've lost their connection.

It's like your body. Your body has blockages that can develop. You need to find a way to unblock these things so that your arms and legs work right. It's the same in your life. We're not aware that we're blocked over there. Then you get stopped. You can't move forward, with doubt, with fear.

Sometimes it's anger. People get angry, too angry. I know that we used to win Slahal games by making the other side angry at us. Because they'd lose their connection to their personal power. But most of us are unaware of this process, right?

What I found, anyway, where I get my strength from, it all comes from the same place: the Creator. That's where it comes from. Some people sit in the sweat lodge and that works for them. Some people go to church, and they sit and pray. The Shaker Church gives them faith, it gives them conviction, it gives them strength.

When we are in need of something, the universe responds. The Creator responds. And the way that we talk to God—talk to the Creator—is through prayer. So that's what we do. That's how I get my strength, is prayer. But you have to calm your mind. You have to be aware of some of the blockages that exist.

When I started doing burnings, the old man told me, he says, "You're a young man. People are gonna come up to you and say, 'You've got no right to do that'" [he laughs]. That's a blockage, you see? You'll have to disregard that, because you're the only one who can say, "I'm gonna go now. I have to do this." So, I had to do it. But that's a blockage, you see?

And all of us have these blockages to the honest connection—what I call the God connection. And you have to know that they're there. And you have to try to eliminate them, these blockages, which are fear, doubt, hatred. And these are all things that block you from your God connection. All of the spiritual training that we do with people is by eliminating those things. It's called growth. And when we tell people that we want you to grow, that's what that means.

Many of the elders I've known, they had it. And it's something that each and every one of you can learn, anybody can. Sometimes it takes lifetimes, though. More than lifetimes, and that's okay. The Creator understands that, so they send you back to do it again [he laughs]. "Try it again!"

And I say, "Okay, I'm here. I'll do it" [he laughs].

"Maybe you'll make it this time."

Then we fail, and that's okay. Do it again. God loves us all so much, I feel. And he put us in this place—to learn, to make choices that he places in front of us every day. And he'll continue to put stones and lessons in front of you until you learn, until you apply it yourself, until you teach it to others. That's why we're here.

GWEN I think it's special what Steven is saying. And it's true. It's where you get your strength from. And I shared earlier our connection to our culture, and our traditions, and spirit. And all I know is that from a very young girl, I knew what spirit was and that it's good.

And we've been teaching our children and our grandchildren to see the good. Don't look at the people, because sometimes they're angry and hateful and all those things we mentioned. Look at the good. Look at your aunties that love you. Look at your uncles that care about you. Look at the good. Don't look at the bad. I tell them, "If you're angry, don't get angry. Because if you're angry, it's just like a leak in your body. You're losing your energy. And it weakens your body and it weakens your mind."

I taught my grandson when he was young. When something frightened him, and he was going to take off, I grabbed him, and I held on to him. I said, "Don't ever run. Don't ever get so afraid that you can't think. Don't get so scared or afraid that you can't think. Because that's when you'll get hurt."

Staying in control or awareness is the first thing we learn. And it's true that we learn about prayer, and I say, "We grew up together."

I remember the dream that I had. And there was a psychic lady that came to the valley, and I was invited to go to this home she was at. So I thought, I'm going to share this dream I had with her.

And she was looking at me. And I could tell she could see, but I could see her too. And she knew that too. When I say that, I mean on a spiritual level. She was a good person, but she was real curious.

So I told her, "I'm just going to share this dream I had." I said it was Steven and me, and we were both younger, and I had a child. He had a child too, and we were running up this hill. And the trees were big, and the moss. I could see the moss.

And it was all pristine, just pure. But we're running, and I was afraid, and he was ahead of me. And I heard shots and then I felt something, and I fell on one knee. And he came back, and he looked really concerned. And he was speaking in another language, and he was wanting me to get up and run.

And I said, "I can't." And he was pleading for me to get up. And I said, "No." And then I showed him my side. And he knew, and I knew. I said, "Take the kids." And I told him to go in this other direction. You could hear them coming up the hill—whoever was chasing us—so he grabbed the two kids, and he started going up. And then I got up, and I went as far as I could. And I took a branch, and I brushed his trail, brushed his trail. Then I laid down, and I could hear them getting closer. And I start to cover myself with leaves. Everything's in black, and I died.

So I turned to the lady who I was telling this to, and she was sitting there. She was just crying, right? I'm thinking, "I thought you were a psychic lady" [she laughs]. I want insight. And she just said, "Well, you and Steven have been together many lives. It's not the first time. And you're just back here to do your work." And I'm lucky, and I know. I know that I wouldn't be here if it wasn't for him.

We fasted on a mountain. He was told he had to fast on a mountain. And we'd already fasted several times in the sweat lodges. And it's not easy. By the third day, fourth day, it's not easy.

But the lady was talking to the people, and points at us, and there were more and more people. More and more people, and I didn't understand them. Then the next thing I see is my grandfather sitting there. Except he was all in white—the spirit—but you could tell he had a buckskin coat on. And he was sitting there, and then I had to sit with him, and I was having all of these things shown to me.

So the next day, we're both tired, and hungry, and really, really thirsty. Steven said, "We have a little bit of time. We could find a stream and go swimming" [she laughs]. And I said, "Okay." So we walked. He gave me a stick and he had a stick. Pretty soon he's getting farther and farther. He looked at me, and he was going, "Hurry up!" And I was going, "Slow down" [she laughs]. And we end up hurrying and slowing down and not being able to walk together.

We found a stream and rolled around in it. Mountain Stream is his name, that's my father, Mountain Stream. We had to literally roll in it. It was small. We get all the way back to where we were, and he says, "We have enough time to go one more time if we want." And I said, "Let's go." Because it's water, right?

But anyway, they came the fourth day to break our fast, early in the morning. And Christine, our older daughter, was with them. And she had blankets, and the man said, "We're here to marry you. That's the message your daughter has. You need to get married," in the mountains, shorts on, cold and hungry, but spiritually married in the mountains.

Bottom line is, the spirit shows us every day what to do. It guides you. That's what we've been saying. And exactly what you're doing, you're listening. Exactly what you're doing, you're listening. You're doing what you're supposed to be doing, and it's not easy. Right, it's not easy sometimes? But we do that anyway.

We get confirmations and affirmations. Some people want a miracle. There are miracles every day. Each and every one of you is a miracle. Life alone is a miracle. We're supposed to be spiritual people.

I remember Steven was challenged one time. Other people were saying, "How could you be a political leader and a spiritual leader?" And that troubled him, and it troubled me. And I told him, "Well, let's just ask the spirit." And we both went to sleep.

Gwen values nonverbal communication, often speaking with her hands.

And the next day, when he woke up, I said, "Did you ask?" He goes, "Yeah." And I said, "What did the spirit say?" And he said, "We're all supposed to be spiritual. Our political leaders are supposed to be spiritual. Bankers are supposed to be spiritual. There's not supposed to be no lies. If people were all spiritual, we'd live in a good place because the spirit is good. The spirit is kind. The spirit will guide you."

And we tell the people, it doesn't matter how you pray, everybody needs prayer. And your greatest source of peace, your greatest source of energy, your greatest source of strength comes from spirit. And it's true. There are people who want it. There are people who will take it. There are people who will expect it. But guess what? It's true. And you can have that anytime and anywhere. That's it.

GENE AND WENDY HARRY

MALAHAT NATION

WENDY HARRY We were married in a Catholic church, St. Paul's in North Van [Vancouver, BC], two blocks down from our place.

It was amazing because we had only been together for three months, and we planned our wedding together. We paid for everything together. We bought all the matches with the names. You know how it was, a long time ago? The napkins with our names on there, and balloons with our names on there—all the decorations—and we paid for the hall.

GENE HARRY I worked at a tuxedo shop, so we got a lot of help from the tuxedo shop. I walked eleven blocks to go to work, eleven blocks home. On my way up to work, I'd get a newspaper and have a cup of coffee. And, you know, I never really learned to read and write until a few years ago—eight years ago—when I went to preschool to learn to read and write.

WENDY Mondays and Tuesdays Gene's in preschool. He teaches children and parents. The rest of the week, it's the church, and then he works as a "drop-in elder" with Native Health, with homeless people who are also First Nations and living with HIV. He works from the clinic and on the streets of North Van, walking outreach. A lot of our people are family members but have no family—they can't go home, are not wanted at home, people are scared of them. Gene even used to bring his own knife and fork to work. We just didn't know much about HIV, but of course we do now.

THE INDIAN SHAKER CHURCH

The Indian Shaker Church was started near Olympia, Washington, in 1881 by Squaxin shaman John Slocum and his wife, Mary Slocum. The Indian Shaker Church has nothing to do with the Shakerism of the East Coast. Rather, it is a unique blend of Catholic, Episcopal, and Native beliefs and ceremonies practiced throughout Coast Salish communities. It is not necessary to give up traditional teachings to also hold Shaker beliefs.

Abstinence from alcohol, smoking, and gambling are part of the Shaker faith, which also emphasizes cleansing—"brushing off"—rituals to purify faithful worshippers. Hand bells and candles are used in ceremonies, as well as song and prayer. Ministers often travel long distances when called to "brush off" or otherwise aid practitioners, and to perform marriages, memorials, and other ceremonies.

The faith has spread from South Puget Sound country to Metro Vancouver and throughout British Columbia. —LVM

GENE That was the best part of my life, not knowing how to read. I went to every school on the island and either I was kicked out or I was dismissed because I wouldn't participate. Nobody knew I couldn't speak English. My cousin Roy Daniels's late sister knew, so they always kind of took care of me. I was raised in our language. My mother's grandmother sent me back to her little brother, who lived with his father, so his father raised me. So that makes it my great-great-great-grandfather who raised me, and he didn't speak English.

I really never knew English. I struggled with English. I'm a little bit struggling with our language now because I'm losing lots because of not practicing it. It's coming back though. My friend Willie Seymour really corrected me, let me see that I'd always thought I was an unfit person, an undesired person, that's what I felt. I was ashamed to be an Indian. It wasn't till 1996, he says, "You're a very special person. You've got the language of your grandmother, you've got the language of your parents." He said, "That's all that really matters, what's inside here."

WENDY We met when I was in the longhouse in 1975, and they used to have the new dancers serving the people tea and coffee. We had to do all the work. We had to do all the kitchen work. We weren't allowed to talk to anybody. We just had to do the serving, and the cleaning, and whatever else.

And I was at their table serving them, and I heard them talking, and then this girl walked in from Musqueam. And they were saying, "Oh, look over there." Gene looks over and says, "Oh, is that her? I didn't recognize her with her clothes on." So that was the first time I had taken notice of Gene, and I was like, "Ooooh, god."

Then I saw him again at a casino while I was playing Bingo. He came and talked to me and asked if I went to canoe races. I said, "Yes, sometimes I do." He asked if I was going to Lummi, and I said, "Yes, I go to Lummi," and that was the next time I saw him.

At Lummi, I came with the canoe club, and we were staying at a hotel. I woke up in the morning, and they said, "Hey, Gene Harry's sleeping in the car outside." And I said, "What!?" So, they went and woke him up, and he goes, "Oh, is Wendy around?" He says, "Oh, just wondering what you're doing today [during the canoe race]?" He offered me a ride down to the race and then drove me all around Bellingham and said, "Oh, I'm lost!" So we were riding around all day like that and by the time we got down to the canoe race it had ended. He says, "Oh, I'll give you a ride home." And I'm like, Yeah right. So he drives me home, and we've been together since. Three months later we were married.

opposite Gene at the Squamish Nation Shaker Church, North Vancouver, British Columbia.

GENE I came to a canoe race but didn't get to race that day. I was on the *St. Patrick*. We were hot and cold that year. It was a good year. It was like pretty clean races, no battling. I got the tail end of the *St. Patrick*, and we'd win a couple, lose a couple, win a couple.

The strange part was, we'd win Saturday, and I'd be out celebrating, and they'd take me off, and they'd have a battle. Then that following week, we'd train real hard and win again Saturday easy, and Sunday I never made it to championship. I was always left off because I was crazy. I kind of had to let everything go because my mother-in-law didn't want me to drink.

WENDY I was just thinking about that. Yeah, he was crazy. It is so true that love is blind. We were only together the three months before getting married. I didn't see it in those three months. And then we were married, and about seven months later I was seeing that he had a drinking problem.

Gene has been a minister at Squamish in North Vancouver, British Columbia, since 1987.

GENE It wasn't a beer-bottle drunk. It was a whiskey—Black Velvet. I don't know why, don't know where that comes from. I smoked cigars, and I couldn't give it up. I heard from a great man that canoe pulling and training interfered with his drinking. I said, "I wish." I said that. It is so awesome that I still, after almost fifty-eight years, am part of it.

There was a ceremony happening and somebody asked me to go behind the curtain, and I was so happy to go behind the curtain because that was the only thing I wanted in life, to be a masked dancer in the smokehouse.

So when I went behind the curtain, and it wasn't to be with the mask, it was to deal with a relative who's gone now who was a clown, and he wanted me to walk with him. And I said, "Oh no, you guys walk by yourself, make a fool by yourself, and you guys make everybody laugh by yourself. You don't need me."

"Oh, do you have any pointers?" he asked. So I gave him some pointers: playing around masked dancing as a clown, shuffling, bugging the ladies, asking for more money, smelling the money, doing all kind of things as a clown.

So then, *boom boom boom boom boom*! The ceremony started, and I was stuck behind the curtain, and I was really mad. Everybody went out. I missed the masked dances. I missed my relatives dancing, and I missed everything. Pretty soon, I could hear the people talking, laughing, having fun. I was so mad at the clown because he made me miss everything.

He was so happy he got a blanket, gave me the blanket, just gave me everything that he had, just, "Thank you, thank you, that was the best ceremony I went to." Sooo, when I came out, I had the blanket. I had the money and all the gifts. And my mom got mad. She kinda pushed my head, and said, "Don't you ever do that again!" This was all the way home.

The next morning we went on the ferry to Saanich, and I clued in. They thought I was the clown. Auntie and Uncle said, "You come home, my boys will teach you how to dance." So that was when my mom and I got so close together. That's all I needed—her permission, her blessing—and I got it that day. We had fun, and we never spoke English together. My wife would say, "What are you guys saying?" Talking in our language, laughing, and having fun. I was emotional that day, so happy I had a mom.

My mom gave me the Sxwaixwe mask, and I spent more time with her while we went to see all the elders around the territory. First Wilfred and Arvid Charlie knew about it; Arvid was my main source. That was the beautiful part about it. I got to know my mom, and I got the gift that I wanted. My granduncle who raised me, he had that same mask, but he couldn't give it to me because it wasn't his to give to me. My mom had to give it to me. Today a lot of things are going wrong because granduncles are giving the mask to their grandnephews. A lot of things can be misused or misinterpreted.

WENDY When he had the mask they said he had to have the song to go with it. So our daughter had to go to the island, and our elder Philomena Alphonse gave her the teachings. We had to go over there, and she taught her for four days about how to eat, how to pray, how to sing. She had four days of training, and I didn't think our daughter was gonna last because they were strict. They were firm with her, and she wasn't used to that.

But she took it on, our daughter. I was listening. I can't say anything about their masks or their song because I didn't know. And that's the thing too, you gotta marry into the mask, and that's what I was worried about. I do come from the mask on my side, so we're okay, 'cause the mask can only marry from the mask family. That's why they called it a secret society—only they know what they do, nobody else is supposed to know.

The Shaker Church was always in my family too. My uncle Sammy Lewis built the first church. Well, there was one in West Vancouver first. It was from the 1920s to 1957 in West Vancouver where the mall is. That's where the church was,

Wendy remembers the early days with Gene.

and then after that it was gone from 1957 until 1970, and then Uncle Sammy, he was my mom's brother, built one up at Squamish. He became the minister, and then when he passed away, my mom's oldest sister took over, and she became the minister. Then, when she passed on, my stepfather, my mom's husband, became the minister. And then when he passed on, Gene became the minister. The Shaker people vote on it, and Gene was fairly new in there.

He was a menace [she laughs]. My mom, she prayed for him all the time, praying that he would come to church. And then, pretty soon, instead of fighting him, she would work with him. She would say, "I need you to help me bring this and that to the church." So he'd be driving her and bringing stuff, and he'd be standing at the back door, and he said he could hear them praying for him. And this one time he was saltless, without his self, and she still asked him for help, and so he gave her help, and he was standing there, and I guess he was a little too high, and he walked right up there, and he rang the bell. And he said, "I wanna be a Shaker like you guys 'cause it seems like you guys have fun in here. Praise the Lord, Hallelujah." The minister said, "Stand here, no more drinkin', smokin', stealin', and fightin'." He said, "Hoooly shit, those are the best qualities of my life." [Gene laughs.]

Gene shares a vision of healing.

59

Candles and bells
under a cross
at the Shaker church.

And they didn't let him go after he said that. They made him stand. So, he
sobered up in there. Yeah, they really sobered him up, and he never, never went
back again after that [to his other ways].

GENE A lot of years I had horns, so to speak. If it wasn't for my horns, my
halo wouldn't be straight. There you go, I had to learn how to walk the bad stuff
and face my own self before I could teach.

WENDY So 1987 was when he became the minister. Then, it wasn't until not
too long ago that I started working on building a new church, 'cause the church
is way up in Squamish. That's about a forty-minute drive from West Vancouver,
and it is not the best. So I started working on building a church down in North
Van, and I got a committee together, and it took us four, five years of meeting,

contacting people, getting donations. I didn't realize when I applied to the trust for $180,000, wanting a church like up at Squamish, just the four walls and a floor—I didn't realize that being in the city, we would have the building codes, and when the contractors came in to do the budgeting it was like $500,000, but we got it built.

GENE We also travel and do marriages. I like to create happy times to make it even sound better, the wedding party. I always tell the man, when the lady puts her hand down there, and he puts his hand down on hers, "Have a good look at that, take a picture, 'cause that's the last time this man is going to have the upper hand" [he laughs].

The most memorable wedding was having two dragon boats tied together. We went out under the Lions Gate Bridge, and the couple came paddling in on an outrigger, and the bride got out. By the time we finished, we were in front of the lighthouse, drifting back in with the tide. I get asked at weddings to do more weddings. I was at this wedding and this one says, "Wanna do my wedding?" I say, "Yeah, when is it?" And he says, "I still need to find a girl!" [he laughs].

WENDY I told Gene, "You can travel wherever you want. All I want from you is pictures, and I want you to keep a journal of all your journeys so that the kids can read it." So he went to Phang-Nga, he went to Malaysia, he went to Singapore, he went to Hong Kong, he went to the Philippines, all for dragon boat racing.

GENE In North America, we were undefeated—Chicago, Philadelphia, Montreal, San Diego—and we go overseas, and we're always second. The closest we came to being world champions was nine inches.

Candle on a small altar at the Shaker Church.

I traveled to India to stay with His Holiness the Dalai Lama for a month. Two years later, I went back, His Holiness wanted me to come back. When His Holiness went back to India, he had the man who takes care of him with him. He took us to Tibet to meet his family. We almost got arrested, because one of our group had a book, and it had the old Tibetan towns by their old names that had been destroyed. One of the chiefs mentioned the name of the village by the old name, and so they were stuck for about five hours before they were let go. Luckily the person with the book had the receipt from the Library of Vancouver, so they kept the book and let us go.

WENDY They brought His Holiness up to the mountains when he was here—to the mountains in our territories—to show him our lands up there. Gene said he learned His Holiness attracts sponsors, and that's how he feeds the orphans in India—the ones that people drop off at the monastery, because they can't raise them. Their families can't feed them. At the monastery they teach the children about the Tibetan ways, different training. There is one where they go into a cave for forty-nine days—forty-nine days of darkness, no talking. So that's part of their training. Some of the sponsors pay to do that themselves. It changes their auras.

GENE You see lights in your hands after so many days. When you clap, and it's like a sparkler. Then you define seven years—seven lights—'cause you start to see seven lights on your body.

WENDY It's like the chakras [the energy points in your body, according to yoga].

GENE And when you do hands-on healing in "the Shake" [the Shaker Church], that's what they say, you're balancing the chakras. We didn't know that, until we compared it with Rosalyn Bruyere's teachings. She taught chakra balancing in California for seven years, and she came to North Van, and she worked on some of our people, and they compared. The nation used to bring her to the Squamish Nation, with all the healers that follow her. We have some in Edmonton, Calgary, Victoria, Vancouver. She would just put a call out. They would all come to the gym, all bring their mats. Then the people would just come in and line up, and they would do the chakra healing.

I was brought by the elders to the Shaker Church and to a medicine man. I became paralyzed. I was suicidal when I was young. When I got paralyzed, some people thought—and I was hearing it being said—I should go into a hospital, a home. I didn't want to be in any of those facilities, and so I thought of many ways to take care of myself. They brought me to Shaker Church, but I had no use for

opposite Gene at home with family.

63

God. And then they brought me to a medicine man, and he sang a song. I got up and I danced with him. I fell down when he stopped, and he laughed, and I was mad 'cause he was making fun of me. He sat me down and said in our language, "He's got it, he's got it. Oh no, no, *ahwo*, it's got him." It got me. And then he sang a song again. He stopped, and I fell down again. He laughed, and he said, "He's strong. It's got him, and it won't let go now. It's got him."

He was laughing, and I was thinking he was making fun of me, and he sat me down again. He did the same thing—stopped—and I fell down, and he sat me down.

He said, "Do you want to see this boy walk again?" And the older one said, "Yeah." My sister said, "Yeah, I want to see him walk."

Then he picked up his coat and had me walk out. Then we were at his house. They were talking, talking, talking. They forgot I understood everything in our language. "Which Big-House we gonna put him in?" they asked.

And then my sister said, "Oh yeah, we got strong ties, Victor Underwood will

Gene works as a minister to people who struggle with conditions such as drug addiction, AIDS, or housing insecurity.

DOWNTOWN
EASTSIDE PHARMACY

take him." Oh no. I didn't want to be anywhere, in any smokehouse. I went to this little island. Then they said, "We know you're not healthy. Build a tent for so and so." I was paralyzed, but I helped build a tent for Freddy Mitchell. Then they said, "Dewey's? Going in. David Sylvester? We need one more tent."

I was just a hammerman. So I built that tent, and I said, "Oh, I have time to catch the next ferry and get off the island." And I opened the door and [he claps his hands together] they picked me up and put me back in there. I built my own tent [laughing].

And then when I went, I was initiated into this beautiful Seowyn, our traditional spiritual practice. The only ones that took care of me were people who spoke the language. "Don't be loud." They said, "Don't be loud because if you're loud, you're gonna be 'yakkity yak yak yak yak yakkity yak.' You're gonna know everything. Stay low but 'Oh oh oh Seowyn' [loud]. Bring it up to the roof, your

Gene's work as a minister brings him out of the church and onto the streets where most of his congregants live.

65

Seowyn"—and now you never hear nobody say that. They want them to be louder and louder and louder. "I can't hear you!" That's not my teaching.

I was the only one who could sit in the chair like this, 'cause I was paralyzed. When I wasn't dancing, I was paralyzed. They had to tie my hands to the pole.

Every time I went to the Big-House I had to be at the end, and I had to lean on somebody. I wasn't spoiled, but I got anything and everything. If they were eating ducks, I ate ducks. If somebody was eating fishhead soup, I got fishhead soup. If you were having a cup of coffee, I'd have some of your cup of coffee. They said, "Hey, that's Big-House food." I asked, "Hey, what is this?" They said, "Big-House food." That ain't no Big-House food where I'm from.

Ducks, fishhead—I even had dried clams in my pocket. We never went in the kitchen to eat. We always stayed in the Big-House. When we did cover-up, we didn't cover up like this for memorial. They just put a scarf here and here. We still could see, so I just closed everything. Most of the time I closed my eyes 'cause I hated being a dancer, until our hats came off and I could say, "Hallelujah, I'm proud to be a dancer." And I could move my arms, and I could run. It wasn't until our hats came off that I said, "I'm glad I'm a dancer." And I thought, Damn, I wish I said that as soon as I got my hat. I still fought it.

above Gene holds a candle to place on the altar.

right A prayer bench sits below the altar.

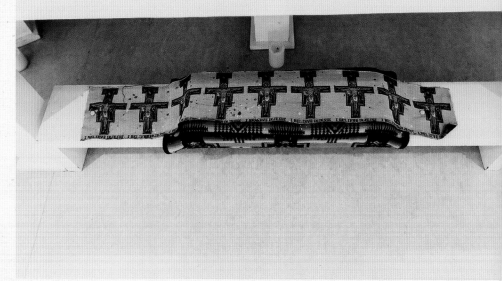

For ten days I never ate (at my initiation), and I was so mad I was a dancer. The meal was there. The late Auntie Rose James said, "You make the sign of the cross first, son, before you eat. Give gratitude for the food." And I had no use for God, so I just watched everybody eat, and I starved.

By the eleventh day, I was sooo hungry. The food came in [repeatedly crosses self]. I couldn't stop doing this [making the sign of the cross]. I wanted to eat! When they said I get to eat duck, and they put the ducks in front of us, and they were supposed to put a mark on there first. Well, once it was at the table, to me it was free-for-all [rubs hands together], and I ate the whole duck, leaving just the bones, and it was dripping out of

A statue, candles, and bells on the main altar of the Shaker Church.

my hand. The Indian doctor came, "Ahhaaaaaaa," and everybody came. "He ate the whole thing!" She pulled up my shirt, marked my stomach. "I neeever did this before, but I'm gonna work on the duck inside you. I hope it works. You're not supposed to eat till we bless it!" So that's when I learned how to make the sign of the cross, full stop, and just enjoyed my meal.

Sometimes people used to get mad at me because how they work today is pretty rough, and I said, "You know that's residential school stuff. Nooobody hurt me when I went in. They sang a song." They sang their song, wherever they had me, and if I was quivering and shaking and went to sleep, they were gentle. They never jolted me to wake up. Once, I fell asleep, I was sitting on a rafter, watching myself go around and around and around—that's an out-of-body experience. And the beauty of those men that were blowing on me in winter. The song is still here [points at his head] where they were blowing, and the song is still here [points at his heart] where they were blowing, their song is still here, still here, and still here. I was wrapped like a baby. I was treated really, really with high respect. When they held me, it was high honors and there was no jolting.

Now I understand the old people. They said, "The dead people, our ancestors, connect with us through the initiation of the longhouse. The song is the same."

You take gentle care when you put somebody in the Big-House, and they'll have the purity and the power of the song. And it never leaves them, when you put your song into them. And they'll own it. Moving away the ugliness I had in my body and replacing it with their breath, that's going to be there forever. So now it's opening season for the Big-House to be open. I could feel those guys—that blowing on my neck, those who sang their song—and I only have one left of my workers. They're all up at that happy hunting ground now. Gentle care, that's the beauty of the old people.

People I always would see said, "I want Willie Seymour to speak for me. I want Will Seymour to do this for me, to do that," because he had so much knowledge, and he had so much freedom of giving you something to walk by, to be strong by, and to anchor us for who we are. He would say, "The wind blows, but we'll never be uprooted. Can move around, but we'll always be anchored to where we come from."

My wife really liked to listen to Willie's stories. He'd end it, and we'd be puzzled 'cause he'd make us figure it out [he laughs]. "I'll be back next week to finish it." It'd be some stories that were so awesome about him growing up with his grand-parents. He lived that gift of being raised by his grandparents. I'm honored to say we're in the same family tree. That's why he took care of me. He always called me little brother, little brother, little brother.

Gene exits the Shaker church where he serves as minister.

SHAKER CHURCH
104 MATHIAS

Willie Seymour, he talked about the first-born, the second-born, the third-born, and the fourth-born. The first would always go to the parents of the father.

The second child goes to the parents of the mother. And it is not necessarily that we lose them. We often still raise them, but the teachings are handed down in this way.

And it's like, it wasn't pick-and-choose, but that's just the law of the old people. They want to give their gifts to this child. It's under the wings of their grandparents, then parents, then aunties and uncles that they learn everything. So that was it, taking a community. That's why Willie said, "It takes a community to raise a child," 'cause everyone will claim somebody, somewhere.

When I was growing up Willie corrected me, 'cause I said, "I feel like I'm not wanted." And my uncle Vincent claimed me three times.

Willie Seymor was so awesome when he said, "Words are a feast." I'm still trying to struggle with that. "Words are a feast." It fills you up. How do you get a feast out of words? And then one time we were working on the floor together. There was a teaching the younger people wanted to bring out, and we were working on the floor. And Willie said, "This is unheard of by our people. I have no words for what they wanted us to do. I have no words for it in our language. So I'm gonna stand beside you and am going to see what you know about it."

So, that's as far as we got. That kinda relates to, going back to one of the things that I was puzzled about. At my home, Malahat, it's forbidden to have the casket open after six o'clock. And that puzzled me, because as a little boy I witnessed no coffins. You're wrapped in a blanket. So if it was all blanket, your whole body was showing. Then once your face was covered, they buried you or stuck you in the tree. That was one of the things I asked Willie about, to help, nurture me with his words. In our area sometimes the coffin is open from nine thirty till close to midnight, 'cause the people come to pay their respects, and relatives will say, "Oh, you're teaching them bad things. Who are you? You should know better than that."

And I said, "I'm just gonna lay a few words down. What you see, if it's not in your heart, you just watch and listen. It's the community's healing, how they are. And if you are scared of what you're gonna see, there's the door, go stand outside for a while until our ceremony's done." Each tribe has something different. And Willie always said, "I haven't tasted this teaching yet." So, I know and kind of understand. It's a "feast." The teachings are a feast. And he was just so magical with his words.

You know, I feel bad 'cause when we were younger, just because we were on different canoes, I wanted to beat him so bad, and he was so like, "Hah." You know, Willie Seymour was a champion on *Mount Prevoe*. He was a champion

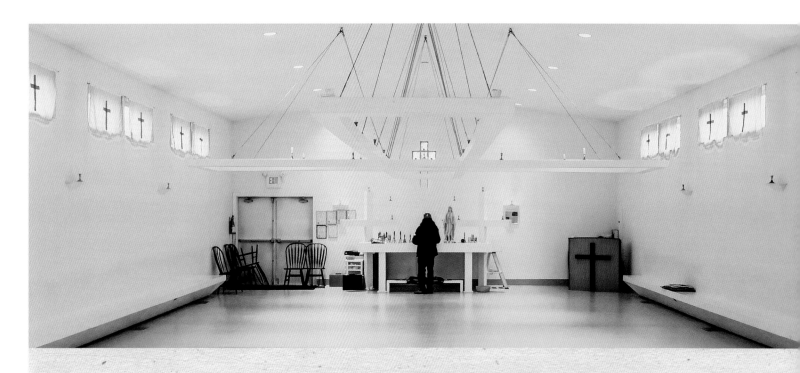

on *Shadow*. He was a champion on *Rainbow*. He was a champion on *Geronimo*, *Cowichan Queen*, and he was a champion on *Five Star*.

And he never bragged about it. He was so humble. We paddled together and one time he said to me, "I'm feeling bad. I think your boys are going to kick me off 'cause I'm too fat." And "Oooh," I said, "if they take you off, Willie, I'll get off too." So when they took Willie off, I got off, never went back. I felt him. I felt his pain. But when we both got off, they had a hard time. You just go until you can't go no more.

He gave me a lot of good teachings. He comforted my spirit and made me realize that there's no such thing as adoption, but you've been picked up as a gift. You'll get greater gifts from someone else. And that's soooo beautiful. I wished I was as smart as he was, but he still felt that he didn't fit, still felt that he was lonely. He said, "I'm sooo lonesome even in a room full of people."

Sharing his words has given to me a shaking up inside, 'cause I now understand the language is soooo important. We have to walk it, talk it, and now I know that the "fill us up with it" is with love and compassion. To love yourself, to be able to love who you and your surroundings are, he always told me, "You love your enemy, because maybe you're in the room by yourself," he said, laughing. I had a hard time with that one: "Love your enemy." A lot of magical words he said to me.

The majority of Willie Seymour's life he was a champion. Wow, and you never knew it. So humble about it. He's been gone about two years now. His memorial will be a full house.

GENE HARRY First we're going to say thank you for being here. Now, the work is going to roll. Now, we're all at attention, honoring spirit, honoring life, honoring the world. Prayers . . . It's most valuable. It doesn't just belong to certain people. It belongs to everyone who takes care of each other, and it is why we're here today.

Our young people are going to walk for a moment, boarding a plane to the other side of the world. They're going to be taking care of our feelings, of the elders' feelings, the great-great-grandparents' feelings, and show the world on that side how important and how valuable this world is. So that's why we're here. It's the surrounding and the protection of the younger people who are making that journey and moving this word to the other side.

Huli:ta'tum uhw
Huli:ta'tum uhw
Huli:ta'tum uhw
The world is alive, the world is alive.

This is the gathering that we're here for—to take care of their minds, their spirits, that they get there safely. To show to the people there that our ancestors knew how to value the world.

The world was on fire, then the fire settled down. Then came the water, the waves. Then came the land. Then came the people, the people. All they had to do was promise they would take care of this land, because the Creator said, "You come from the earth, from the dust of the cedar." Our ancestors promised to take care of this land and only take what we need. That's what the children are going to bring for us.

Friends and relatives, this earth who is our mother, like everyone, has a story of creation. These beautiful, beautiful trees represent our mother, our ancestors— where we come from. Stories say the Creator made everything that flies first in this world. Then he created everything that comes from the mountain—the four-legged, the insects. Then he created everything that belongs in the sea.

Then he created a community of people. Picking up some beautiful red powder from a giant cedar tree, he sang a song, as our songs go in prayer, and he blew in the palms of his hands and that dust settled.

One of those stars touched that dust, and that cedar dust settled, and there was the first chief. He did the same thing, the cedar dust dropped, and there were our elders. He did the same thing, and there was the family of children, mothers, and fathers. And he went to a younger tree, and he said, "Take care, only take care, use what you have to, take what you need," and the teaching that went from this.

Huli:ta'tum uhw
Huli:ta'tum uhw
Huli:ta'tum uhw
The earth is alive
The earth is alive
Truly, the earth is alive,
The People are still here.

CLAUDE WILBUR

SWINOMISH TRIBE

I was born here, at Swinomish, named Kuts-bat-soot. My grandfather Charles A. Wilbur was into politics, as was my father, Tandy William Sr. My dad did a lot of that stuff. He knew all of the old-timers. They got a lot of things done for Lummi and Swinomish—a lot. My father did a lot of that work. He wasn't much of a fisherman. He was a better politician. But he had a boat and had a toot-along engine. He would crank it by hand to start it. We called it a put-put.

SALMON IS A WAY OF LIFE

Among Coast Salish people salmon is more than a food, it is a way of life. It is beatitude, a form of wealth, a tie to home waters, and food for the spirit. "Feed your Indian" is the saying. It starts with salmon.

To be a fisherman is not a job; it is a lifelong identity that starts at an early age.

Before reserved treaty rights to fish were affirmed by federal court decisions, tribal members fished not only to provide for their families but because that was who they were. Later, fishermen dragged their catch through the grass, hiding it from game wardens, who would administer not only tickets but also beatings. The fishing continued. There was never a thought or possibility that it would not continue.

Today some fishermen invest in expensive boats and travel for commercial fishing, while others fish only occasionally for ceremonial purposes—for halibut, herring, shrimp, clams, crab, black cod, geoduck, and more. And always, salmon, whether Chinook or silvers or chum or sockeye, cut into crimson fillets and roasted on sticks by a fire, or canned, smoked, or made into soups or cakes.

A good fish cook is always in demand and will travel all over to cook for ceremonial events where there is only one food that will do: salmon, cooked just right with a good crust that seals in the juices. The experienced cook knows how to gauge just right how close to put the stick with its skewered fish to the fire.

A good cook travels with his or her own knife and sharpening stones, and leather to hone the knife to a perfect finish, to make it possible to cut fillets with precision.

These are arts learned over a lifetime, passed down from family to family, from cook to cook, fisherman to fisherman. —LVM

Claude Wilbur.

Claude is a US military veteran and lifelong hunter, fisher, and net-weaver.

I named my boat the *Three Ls* for my daughters: Laurel, Lona, and Lisa. And I also had two boys. Five kids. One of the boys was here last night. Their names are Jimmy and Claude Jr. My mother's name was Laura Warren. There's some Chinese in her family and she came from the other side of Edmonds. All the old-timers at Lummi were fully familiar with my dad, and my grandmother had her relatives up there too. That was her picture there, that little tiny one there [he gestures]. She had relatives at Lummi, my grandmother.

The Lummi and Swinomish have been good friends over the years, good friends. I spent a lot of time up at Lummi. I know lots of people there. Yeah, I ran out there the other day, and my grandson, Tim, from Lummi asked me about this interview. I spend a lot of time over at Little Bear. Some are our relatives, too. So, we're all related. As I say, friends forever.

I learned to fish right here at Swinomish at the slough, just on the other side. There's fishing on the other side. It's called a slough. The straightaway for water-

flow, in and out, water out of the Strait of Juan de Fuca. We did a lot of fishing here. The tributary is the main one to the Skagit River. The Skagit has a lot of good fish, like the Nooksack. Lummi and Swinomish people are lucky to have that place to work. They make good use of it.

I fished my whole life. I was just a youngster, a little one, and I was on a boat before I should be. I never came close to drowning myself, but I did fall in a few times.

I turned out to be a commercial fisherman. I had three boats, one or two too many. They got the best of me. No, they didn't get the best of me. I got the best of them, 'cause I finally quit, but I paid my dues to do that stuff. Everybody has trouble nowadays.

After I started growing up, I put a few years in. I fished the river. The fish used to go this way up the slough, and as a kid I lived up the slough about a couple miles. And we fished out here. My dad, he wasn't a fisherman. He was more of a politician, and he kind of left that boat down there. I took that out and fished with it and caught fish. That was my real start. In the old days, it was rowboats. I lived in that area and everybody rowed.

Skagit Bay is good for drifting too, after you learn the tides. Yeah, a lot of fish. They started arresting us in the Skagit. I spent a couple Thanksgivings in jail for fishing. But pretty soon, in 1974, Judge Boldt came along and straightened things out. And he did give us good fishing times, going out on the water and fishing our waters—I often think that all the fish are still from there, from those times the Boldt Decision created. Judge Boldt kind of saved it all for us. We got the news of the Boldt Decision, and that meant fishing time. That decision was for us tribes to catch half the fish in order to uphold our treaty rights. That was a good deal for us. Judge Boldt's decision in 1974 was upheld by the courts in 1975.

The rez goes around toward Anacortes and then you got Launching Point and Flagstaff on the other side, which is all part of the bay. And there are lifelong fishermen, guys like Ray Paul. He showed me how to fish out in the bay, so I learned from the old-timers how to get from one island to the next.

But it was before the Boldt Decision that I was going out to West Beach—out to the naval station—and yeah, there was a lot of fish. This was a whole ten years before the decision; I remember that span. In 1964 we were already doing what Boldt decided in '74—we were fishing the Skagit River in the same fashion. So

Claude in Tokyo, Japan, while in the US military during the Korean War.

Treasured knife
collection.

we were ten years ahead of Judge Boldt. There were some tough years. And it
helped to bring about the Boldt Decision.

I've done all types of fishing. I got to Bristol Bay, Alaska. Salmon is the really
big thing in Bristol Bay. Everyone got salmon. Springtime was herring, and that
was a big deal down here. We were lucky to have herring here at Lummi. We used
to follow them from San Francisco to Alaska, and that was a good early start for
the summer, fishing herring.

I remember my father was a great politician. He was a boozer, but he was a good
Indian worker. And I remember he would go and have coffee time with the judges
and attorneys in Mount Vernon. He would go to a place like the Coordinance
Club and have coffee with the mayor and the judges. So when he's stooping for
a judge, he wasn't exactly unknown. I could get that help tremendously to get
a favorable decision from the Mount Vernon judges. And they approved of our

78

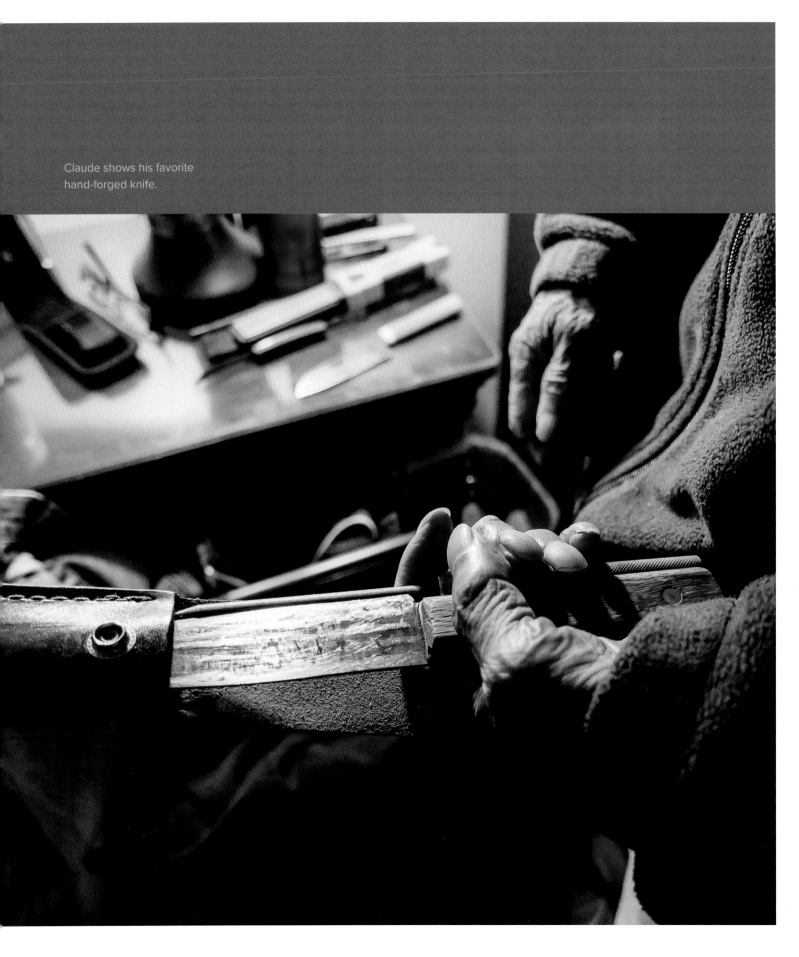

Claude shows his favorite
hand-forged knife.

Claude with grandson
Timothy Ballew, fisherman
and former chairman
of Lummi Nation.

fishing in Skagit River. And fishing, we went. We had many good, prosperous years. No more jail for me [he laughs]. Yeah, there were good years too.

I was just talking to a guy this morning, and he said he knew my grandfather Wilbur, and they fished. They all fished in common. I was having breakfast, and he came up to me and he said, "I knew your grandfather." And I said, "I don't know that was entirely possible, it was probably my father." And he said, "I fished with him. We fished together." Stuff like that. That was pretty neat. People here want to meet a lot with you. That's good, the way it's supposed to be.

I never went into the smokehouse for ceremonial upbringing while growing up. The US government, Bureau of Indian Affairs, made it stop, doing the ceremony and stuff, and we started to go to school. It was the educational push, and when you went to school, they pushed you to go to boarding school and drop your ceremonial stuff.

They must have run into it at Lummi too, where they made you stop doing the smokehouse stuff, so we kind of lost that tradition. But we did keep on going. A couple of our kids have joined up later in life. They got into it and are keeping it going. I think the government gave up trying to make our people stop, I hope.

I served in the Korean War. I got one little tiny picture. I'm standing in Tokyo. Tokyo don't look like it, but there I was. That's me. Nothing has ever much been said about stuff that I did in the war. I gave them a war story when I went in and then I paid for it, after I got to Japan. I kind of halfway teased them, "I'm an Indian Scout, you know?' I did lead the hunt, was a great hunter.

So I told the army how good I was at being a hunter, and I paid for it when I got into a thing called the R&R Platoon, route reconnaissance. What they did was, I don't know if you heard of them or not, but they were known for their scouting duties, and when they had a place to pull over and advance, R&R went first. They scouted the way and checked out the route that the group would take later. That was their job. I did that, and I got a Bronze Star Medal for doing that.

Now, I'm paying the dues, is what I call it. It's all worth it. Lots of people taking care of you.

Except for my time serving in the Korean War, my whole life I fished for gatherings and cooked. Yeah, since I was young in the 1930s and 1940s, cooking with Al Sampson and Lizzy Sampson was in full swing then. We had great times. I had lots of fun with Al playing at the firepit. He was a big man. He was strong. He could throw me around easy. But as a young kid, I liked to play around. They would say something about cooking, "Are you coming down or what?" Yeah, I think I made it easier for them.

Lizzy and her husband, Al, they taught me. He smoked fish and taught me how to make a fire in the smokehouse that burns all night. And so I learned a lot from the old-timers. And Louise Joe and Lizzy Sampson, they were good cooks. They used slow fire, just so much heat.

Lizzy did the cooking, and she did a fabulous job. She had a nice way of cooking it. She used alderwood sapling for her grill. I guess those were the first days. She taught me a lot about cooking fish. And Al, who was a fireman, he tended to the fire, and Lizzy taught us to butcher with the big butcher knife. That's the only knife she used and the only knife I used in my lifetime. I swear by that knife.

Al and Lizzy had to have the fire a certain way, and I learned a lot about fires from them. Al sure knew how to smoke fish. For hard smoking fish, he used old dry maple. It will smolder and smoke the whole night long. Even if the fire goes out, it will smoke. He made good smoked fish, that and barbecued fish. I learned how to take care of a fire from him and the butchering part from her. That's the big reason I have their pictures. I love those pictures.

Claude has spent much of his life weaving, selling, and trading fishnets.

Claude laughs.

Our fish were always at least a hundred pounds. You got up to four or five hundred pounds on the big ones. There was a lot. I couldn't count the numbers of pieces to a fish. It was too hard to do. But it was six or eight pieces on a stick—six or eight servings. So you can see a hundred pounds is quite a few pieces on sticks.

Any size gathering raised its due. They have some big gatherings, huge gatherings. We come out for powwows and whatever they're celebrating. There's a picture of Lizzy inside the smokehouse, cooking [he gestures]; there's twenty-some sticks right there. If they contained five pieces to the stick, five times twenty is one hundred servings.

Yeah, we did all those big gatherings, Swinomish Days and Stommish canoe races. Coupeville canoe races were slightly before my time. Those are Coupeville pictures on the end [he gestures]. The one with the black frame is Swinomish people. My grandfather is in it, so that's a pretty old picture. The others are Canadian. I always kind of favored the Canadians. They came down here on their canoes, and they'd go by our house, which is down on the slough. So sometimes we'd meet them at a place near our house, which happened to be a stream coming up, and it had fresh water. And they could stop and camp and get fresh water right there where we lived.

Yeah, I remember the Tulalip canoe races. They have a really good protected area to canoe race down there—a good place. I have cooked a few times down there, but they had their own cooks. I don't know how I got in—I just like to cook, I guess. I like their fishing area. I did a lot of my fishing down in Tulalip waters. It was a good place to fish. I got kicked out a couple times. I had to fish on the Swinomish Reservation. I had to stay on our side of the reservation line. They had no qualms about kicking me off [he laughs]. "Get out!" [he laughs again].

Fishing up in Canada is an absolute no-no. They are pretty tough, those border police guys. I got caught once. I don't know why I did it—just to defy them, I guess. I was crazy going over the line. It was up by the ferry docks. It's easy to get over the line. I didn't have to go to jail, but I had to go to court. It cost me a couple hundred dollars.

We would go to cook salmon all over Seattle and out to the East Coast. I went out to the East Coast, and that was just a huge thing out there, to have us cook salmon in our traditional way. But Seattle was for the bigwigs. One time we cooked salmon for the governor. Bigwigs like that—town mayors and so forth.

They went along with Indian-style smoked fish. And you can cook it in such a way, and the right way for the fish, put a crusty texture to it, and it'll seal in the juices. The juices will stay in. You don't get a dry cook. You get a really moist texture, and it makes for a really good meal. Kind of a nice way to cook fish—delicious [he laughs].

Most all Coast Salish tribes cook fish. It's just the method that they use can differ. I went up and down the coast, like to the Makah. They like to cook it a little differently than we do. And that's a good way too because it's about how close you put the stick to the fire, so it's a good way.

I don't know when my next cook will be [he laughs].

I make fish sticks. That's me making fish sticks [he gestures to another picture]. I'm still sharpening knives. I have a bunch of sharpening stones in the package. I just touch 'em up. They all work, different gadgets. My boy, he buys knives, like our boys do. They all work once you get the hang of it. I like leather. I use leather a lot, to finish it right.

These are sharpening stones [he gestures to another picture]. I like it better when they're wet. I don't have my favorite butcher knife here, my favorite one. Most people use this type of knife for filleting. It's a favorite for most people. This big one, though, it's all I ever used. My old lady, that's what she used. They say it won the West—that's the rumor about that knife, so that's the one I use.

I got a lot of knives. The women, they try to take my knives away.

RICHARD SOLOMON

LUMMI NATION

Imagine all the pain a heart can handle. That's the story of my grandma's life when she was a child. Eight years old, she lived in the longhouse, out at Madrona Point on Orcas Island in the San Juans.

The sickness, smallpox, came from contact with Europeans. It hit all the Indian people. She said the people started dying, blistering all over their bodies, and they didn't know what it was. All the Indian doctors, they couldn't fix it. She said they had five Indian doctors gathered, trying to figure out why people were dying.

She said there weren't enough people in the longhouse to keep it going any-

THE EPIDEMICS

Before the Indian Wars of the United States, before treaty making and treaty breaking, and white settlement and dispossession, before any of that, came the greatest violence of all against the aboriginal peoples of the Pacific Northwest. Disease.

The Native peoples of the Northwest had no resistance to diseases carried by Europeans and other non-Indian visitors and settlers. Measles. Influenza. Smallpox. The arrival of Europeans on the Northwest Coast beginning in the late eighteenth century marked a collision with a truly alien world and was a calamity without precedent. Disease devastated the Northwest peoples long before white settlement and dispossession began in earnest. On the Northwest Coast, the outbreaks of infectious diseases began in about the 1770s, killing an estimated 80 percent of the Indians there in the first century of contact.

The precontact population of coastal peoples of the Northwest, conservatively estimated at more than 180,000 in the late 1700s, was reduced to only an estimated 35,000 to 40,000 survivors. This was a demographic disaster that shattered Native social and cultural systems and left those still alive traumatized by a terrible death force they did not understand.

The diseases were inadvertently borne on persons, ships, trade goods, and even by Indian family members fleeing infected villages, not knowing they were carrying death to the relatives with whom they sought refuge. The hurt is still there, the bereavement. With not enough people to keep the villages going, people just left. In that way, disease unraveled entire communities. — LVM

more, to keep the fires going, so we left. My uncles were still alive. She said they were mean, that's probably why they lived. She said they were big and tall. She said when our people left, we had to leave the smokehouse, and we gathered our stuff, and we gathered our people from the cemeteries too.

She said that's when I woke up—sitting there in the canoe, with my ancestors wrapped up. We took the ones that still had bodies, she said, and they were all wrapped up. That's when I came to my right mind, trying to remember things and knowing this was real. Sitting with my wrapped-up ancestors.

There's a private museum in Virginia, Hampton University, and also the Smithsonian in Washington, DC. You can go and look at all the stuff from your people. Probably all the stuff, you know, that was taken from the villages a long time ago, when they abandoned all the villages. There's tools, bows and arrows, regalia, baskets, fishing stuff—all kinds of fishing stuff. A lot of the stuff, they don't even know what it was used for. I had to name it all for them.

Richard's partner, Jolene Armstrong, at her desk in their home.

Everything I saw, I knew what it was for. Masks, they had everything. It was kind of sad too, you know, 'cause they had some of our regalia there. They had all kinds of private stuff. Regalia that should've been together were spread apart. They had some Red-Paint canes there that we use to make paint for ceremonial use, it should have gone with the Red-Paint cedar gear. They were listening to me. When I was talking, they followed me around when I was telling them what should be done.

We're taking the relatives so nobody walks on them. I don't want nobody walking on my people. My grandma moved to Baker River, a tributary of the Skagit River, way up by the dam. They went back to the old village on Orcas Island for three years, bringing the ancestors back, taking our people out of the cemeteries. The third year, all the high-class people buried in the canoes and longhouses, they had them in the trees, where we placed them, and they just had been pushed over, and there was people living there. There was no longhouse there at all after three years. She said that was really sad for her and my uncles.

So yes, imagine all the pain a heart can handle. You know the things that they went through to live through that, to even make it through that. She said there were canoes all over the whole Puget Sound like that when the influenza came. Dead people, whole families in the canoes, just drifting around. She said it was like that. That's how bad it was, almost everybody died.

Beads carved by Richard from devil's club.

87

View of the San Juan Islands
from Lummi Nation Reservation shore.

That was her story. I got to learn that story. She brought me to her home, brought me to the places where she camped on her way, telling me about every place she took me to, you know. Her shortcut through Deception Pass was now a raspberry field. That was their slough, their shortcut through there, heading up to Baker River, to the Skagit.

Then she said she had some aunties that went with white men, and they had kids, and I remember playing with the kids myself and never knew what happened to them. I always wondered what happened to them. She always wondered too.

After she got older, after Grandpa passed, she told me Grandpa hadn't been doing good. He was ninety-two years old then. She said to him, "What's the matter, Grandpa? Don't you want to live?" You know what he said? "Oh Grandma, I can't fish for you anymore, I'm no more good, I can't get up the bank. I can't get fish for you anymore. I'm no more good."

What I always think about her, all the time, is how much she talked about the ancestors and the earth. She did that when she was cleaning fish, too. That's when I learned, when she taught me about the salmon. Cleaning fish, she'd tell me about the Salmon People— our people, and other Coast Salish tribes whose lifeways depend on salmon.

Then she always said, "Grandpa always said, 'You better go on over there and listen to Grandma. She's a real Indian.'" Then during that six months she lived after Grandpa passed, she said, "He doesn't talk to me anymore. He used to talk to me. I'm no more good. He talked to me every day, every day at daylight. He don't do that no more. I'm no more good." That's what she said.

The elders must have talked to them a lot, though, for them to live through that kind of stuff that they did. Where do you think we got our memory? Never to forget where we're from. That we're all part of this earth. That we're not the bosses on this earth. A lot of human beings are like that, thinking they're the bosses of the earth. That needs to change. There are some things we have no control over, we have no say. Sometimes the spirit just moves in and pushes us along. We have no say in that, the way the spirit moves.

No matter what we try to do, it still moves us, whichever way it wants us to go. Gives us the strength to do what we gotta do. We're gonna discover that more and more as we go back to the homeland. You know, when sleeping in the villages where our people live, like Cherry Point, Xwe'chi'eXen, and all over, places that we get to sleep where they slept.

The feeling that you get when you sleep there, the things that show themselves when you are there, the spirits that come—I don't know how many times that happened up in Point Roberts. So many things come there, me and my dad had seen, me and my brother had seen, me and my sister had seen. All the canoes that come.

There was a huge reefnet site there at Point Roberts, with seventy or eighty anchor rocks. Some of the rocks with holes in them, in the shallow ends, are still there too. [This is one of the oldest examples of salmon net fishing in the world.] My brother found one out there once and said, "Hey, look here, there's a hole in this rock." Covered in that popcorn kelp. It was in a big rock. The hole was notched in a big rock, where they tied their reefnet. He just happened to see it—the sun hit it just right.

I lived next door to my grandparents, just kind of ended up with them. I was with them all the time, didn't know how lucky I was. They gave me the first candy I ever got, other than that sour old Indian ice cream.

They spoke Hul'qumi'num. Grandma was from Orcas Island. I think they were fishing out there. That's how she got connected with Grandpa. That was a set marriage. I think she was twelve years old when she got married. It's amazing how they set them up for marriage, just because of what that family did, what they knew, where they were located. Everything we have was out our front door.

They went up the Fraser River valley quite a bit, even after the US-Canada border was established in 1818. Grandpa said he and his brothers snuck across to go fishing when they were young. You know, when they put that border in there, it was a really hard decision for the people. It was a really sad story.

Grandma said it was like a one-month deal, you know, deciding where they were going to live. Even though it was just across the way, it was like in Semiah-moo, where they found the bones of our ancestors since then—the border, they just went across the way, people from here.

I will never forget the way Dad was when his last brother died. He was the only one left. He was cooking fish for the burial. He said to me, "Here, I can't do this. I can't do this for my last brother. I'm the only one left." I can't imagine how he would feel. Seven brothers and the only one left, with three sisters. When the youngest daughter passed away, she had a picture of Grandma when she was a child. Nobody knew she had that, and it just came out when they opened the chest that she had under her bed. She had all her stuff Grandma had made her when she was a child. She kept it like brand-new, like a time capsule.

I tell my boy that I always want him to remember where the Salmon People come from, what we learn from them.

opposite Richard carves beads for giveaway.

90

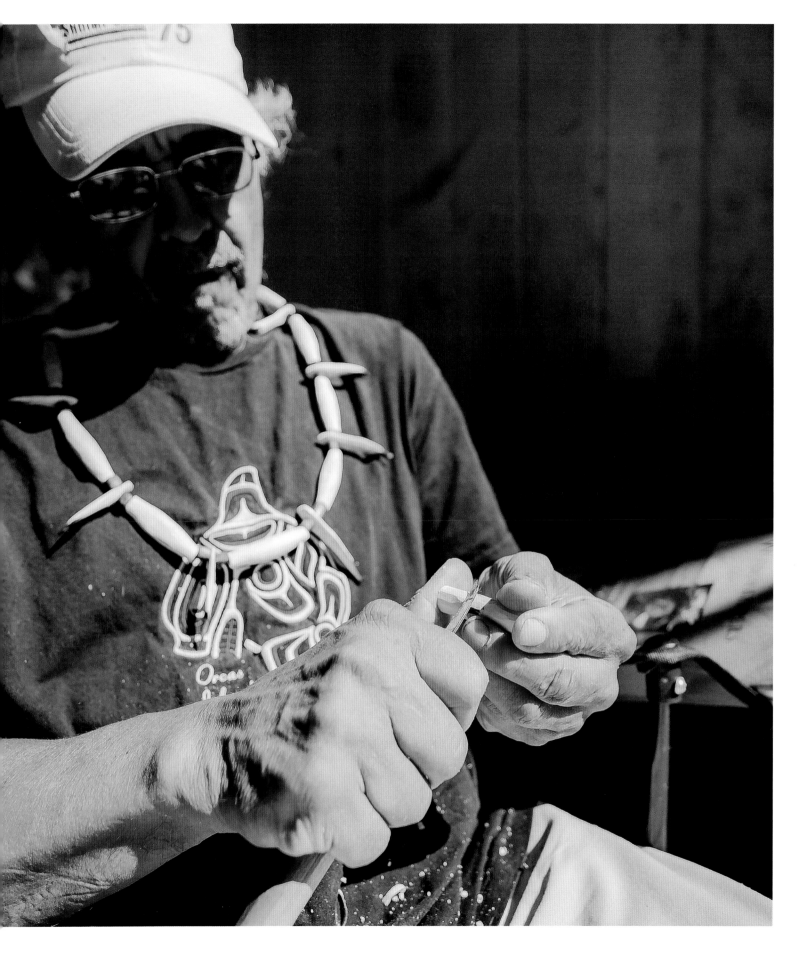

Where do you think we got our memory from? We got it from the Salmon People. The parents do that for their kids, that's how we're supposed to do. That's what I'd like them to remember. I learned that from Grandma. Grandma talking like that, the way she talked about the salmon all the time, how much she respected it. And I always remember that.

I hope we'll get a sockeye salmon season this year. They can't see around that corner, see if we'll get a season. They always think they can, but they can't. Now they're trying to match the science with the stock? They're trying to put a number on it? Everything is interconnected, though, so how can we?

We won the culvert case, again [*Washington v. United States*, requiring the State of Washington to rebuild road culverts to allow salmon to swim upstream, to uphold treaty fishing rights]. It probably won't make a difference at this point. It's kind of sad. They don't respect our treaties. They have so much process on it, processing our treaty to death. It's been debated for 150 years. Now, we have to fight for our water. We should get half the water. We had all the water at one time. Next, we'll be fighting over the air we breathe.

I heard they set some reefnet anchors on top of some old anchors out by Cherry Point, Xwe'chi'eXen, first time in we don't know how long. Look how many years they've been fishing there, look how many of us put them there. Just like out in the islands. They must have tried to keep some of the anchors, but they usually lost the lines on them. They used willow and cedar limbs, and they rotted away, and that's how they lost them.

Larry Kinley, former chairman of the Fisheries Commission, he retired, but now he's over there working on his reefnet more than he ever did before [he laughs], passing his knowledge on to his boys. It doesn't get any better than that. That's what I miss. I miss all my uncles. I thought all my uncles were gonna be here forever. I thought Grandpa was gonna be here forever. He was old when I was a kid, but he was lots of fun to be with. He'd sit on the beach at low tide and say to me, "You'd better get in that water, don't want no stinky Indian next to me."

THE FIRST SALMON

How will we pull our people together, though, tribe versus tribe? The smart people did that. The smart people that we hired divided us, the lawyers, you know. They told us this salmon goes in that river, and this salmon goes in that river, fish DNA—putting up lines.

This is *my* fish, that's *my* fish. What happened to *our* fish? Everybody learned *mine, mine*. Like a seagull—*mine-mine-mine!* Here we are fighting over the last fish on the table. The last meal.

I've been on the Fisheries Commission going on my third term, seven years. Larry Kinley, he's a veteran—just came back to work for a while. Think he's hoping to go fish early kings one more time before he passes away, that's what he says. That's what I was thinking too. You know, 1976 was the last time we got to fish our own kings. We never had to get any fish, you know, frozen fish, or going down the Columbia, or up the Fraser. We should get our own fish.

I'll never forget the first time the tribe tried to freeze some fish—god, Larry was just furious. "What the hell they gonna do, feed 'em some frozen goddamn fish? You go to hell if you go feed me some frozen fish when I die!"

That's the way he said it too. I always remember when he'd get that first salmon. He'd hold it up in the air for his mom: "Look what I got you, Mom. I got this for you, Mom." Grandma would be standing on the dock, but he called her Mom that one time. Only time I ever heard him call her Mom. Otherwise, he'd just call her Grandma. I thought that was a really special occasion.

Salmon People, they go all the way out to the ocean,
come all the way back.
Journey out to the ocean, all the sacrifices that they make,
their people make on the way back up.
And when they come back home, they remember where their home is.
They remember where they live, as they make their way home,
no matter where they're at, where they come from.
All the different rivers around here,
they remember where they come from.
Where do you think we get our memory from?
That's where we get our memory from,
and when they get up there they do the ultimate sacrifice,
for their children. So their children can live.

ELAINE GRINELL

JAMESTOWN S'KLALLAM TRIBE

I was fishing during the good days, and then it turned out to be bad days. I realized too it was a young man's sport or an older man's sport for someone that was much stronger than I. We had very strict rules about fishing. They would come over with that helicopter and want to see me step out there.

I was checked on, as one of the first women out on the Strait of Juan de Fuca to do gillnetting—coho, sockeye. Sockeye, sockeye salmon was the best.

I was there when they took the Elwha dam down in 2011 and 2012. We weren't fishing the mouth of the river then. If you want to hear about the dam removal, you probably want to talk to one of the . . . gosh, they are gone now, too.

I think about our language and I think about the old times, and a lot of the older people are gone now.

WISDOM OF GRANDMA AND GRANDPA

My grandparents made sure I was familiar with our culture—all of our family lines, that I had another side of the family—because that was so important. Grandma and Grandpa were right—how would they know how it would turn out? This is the way I think. Grandpa Dave Prince was a hereditary chief in Jamestown. Grandpa Norbert James was hereditary chief at Lummi. And they both wanted to keep things together in their com-

STORIES ARE TEACHINGS

Stories in Coast Salish country are far more than entertainment. They are teachings, each with a lesson, often a moral teaching: what it means to be generous, or foolish, or selfish, or wise. With theatrics and flair, in storytelling, knowledge and culture are passed on.

Tribes bringing back language also are bringing back stories. Storytelling particularly is emphasized with the young. Some Native storytellers have made a career of it, traveling even internationally to share their culture and stories they learned from their own grandparents.

Told in the old way, some stories take days. So in addition to conveying teachings and vocabulary, stories also teach patience and the art and pleasure of simple presence. Storytime is not screen time. It is time together, time to be attentive and to listen. As old as fire, since time immemorial, stories are at the heart of Coast Salish culture. — L V M

munities. They had that ability to mediate, to think far ahead, with care and forgiveness. You know, oftentimes we forget forgiveness and remember forever the bad things. But you can't. It does something to your soul when you do that.

I remember my folks, my grandma and grandpa Prince, having the first of what everyone calls a "safe house." There was an old jurisdiction. There was a way of mediation to keep people from getting hurt. They had their own police. The family, community system came first.

The person who had the strongest character would resolve disputes—mediate, if you will—and it seemed like both of my grandpas did this. And then, of course, the women gave their voice in there too, to support and take care of whatever they had to take care of, midwifery, all these things. Our community leaders would go into homes where there was disease, and they would take care of it. They'd support both sides, and that caring kept the community together. I think it was a spiritual thing that developed. It's right. You have to do right, be fair, and so they would speak for that.

LANGUAGE, LOST AND RESTORED

Grandma and Grandpa lived with the language, and so I learned the rhythm of the language. But when they would see me listening, or hear me, they would quit talking 'cause they weren't allowed to teach the language. The government told them not to because they thought they could make better white people out of us if they took the language away. And so we lost that. It happened in Chemawa, at the boarding school in Salem. It happened over here at Lummi, too.

But the language is coming back. It's being taught at the high school. Any student can learn the language, whether they're Native or not. In an effort to just hold on to our language, please, somebody, study it. And then it's honored at the University of Washington as a foreign language . . . a foreign language.

The language started out being recorded on microfilm reels, and that progressed to computers. Now, we have a great big book, a grammar book. But the seven people doing that work started dying off. Our last person who died was working on vocabulary. It was a long project. He hung in there. Pretty soon he had his head down on the table, and he stayed that way a really long time. We're all looking at him, wondering, did he fall asleep, did he die? And so we sat there just looking at him. We didn't know what to do. Finally, his wife says, "Are you asleep or what?"

"Oh, I'm just trying to figure this out. First they tell me not to speak Indian: 'Don't do that anymore!' So I forget it. Now, you want me to bring it back?" We had a lot of fun, but all of them are gone now, all seven of them, all good

Traditional halibut hook—the spirit and craft of traditional ecological knowledge.

Elaine on her porch
at S'Klallam.

speakers. They were the people—the root core now—that I was really happy and honored to be around. I could get those feelings from them and solidify the feelings I already had.

When we started the program down at Lower Elwha, ʔéʔɬx̣ʷa, there were seven people that could speak Klallam, Nəx̣ʷsx̌ʼayʼəmúcən. Now there are many speakers from Elwha, ʔéʔɬx̣ʷa, Jamestown, stətíɬəm [like the speaker], and Port Gamble, nəx̣ʷnəx̣ʷqʼíyʼt. They all sound so similar, but they use different dialects like you would have in a place like New York City. You could tell which village they came from, x̣̌čŋin cx̣ʷ čsx̣ʷʔiyaʔ ʔaʔ ʔəyx̣ʷəyx̣ʷəyŋx̣ʷ. So, these seven people were the nucleus of the Klallam language, Nəx̣ʷsx̌ʼayʼəmúcən. But they have passed on, ʔiʔuʔ px̣ʷənəŋ. They were elders, ʔəsʔáyəx̣ʷ, now our ancestors, Sčiʔánəŋɬ. From those seven root people, we now have our Klallam language, Nəx̣ʷsx̌ʼayʼəmúcən, once again.

THE IMPORTANCE OF STORYTELLING

I want to make sure that today all the kids get into the storytelling. Storytelling for me happened a long time ago, during the war [World War II]. We lived alongside the water, and during wartime they had blackout shades, and then you had clips on the side of the curtains, so you can clip those black shades right up against the wall so the light from the house wouldn't be seen from the water. They thought that our enemies were going to come in from the water and land on our beach. So what we did was eat as soon as you could, while it was still light, and then you would get apples. We had a root house, and we stored everything there.

I learned storytelling at a young age, but I didn't utilize it. I thought that was just for me. I thought that was just mine. And I didn't learn until, oh, I was probably twenty-four or twenty-five when I realized that this was for me to give to someone else too—my whole family, you know. These things seep out. They just seep. Actually, I don't know whether you realize how much you really do know until pretty late in life, and that it's important, that I better stick with that, I'm good at that, I'd better continue.

I started in the Port Angeles school district, and now I have carried our stories and songs to Africa, Prague, Bangkok, Japan, and Alaska, way out on Saint Lawrence Island. Africa was fun. I got along really well with the people. They were really interested in Indians. They just really liked the Native Americans. They had thought we were extinct and they were quite surprised when one of us turned up at their hut.

opposite Cedar for weaving.

Elaine shares stories at her home in S'Klallam.

Grandpa Prince would build a fire in the cast-iron woodstove, and those stoves have leaks in them. They're just little openings and cracks, and the firelight would flicker through. So the three of us—Grandma, Grandpa, and me—would sit there, and he would peel apples, and that flame would hit his face, and it would just flicker, and Grandma would flicker. And I'd watch them, and he would tell stories. I was just, ah . . . mesmerized, totally taken in, and I thought, I have to remember.

When you are that grandfather, you have that spirit. That's what was left behind for us. I was that spirit and that innate knowledge for us. We often will see something. It won't turn around and tell us, but we see it, and that's ours, that's part of our spirit, in our heart, and just the way we feel about life, you know. *I can do this. I can do this, and I want you to do the same.* We all know that we have our limitations, but we live with that. Our people have ways to handle our limitations, too. We took them as far as we could, and then they make their choice how best it feels to them, like you will make your own life fit you.

They say if you want to go fast, go by yourself. If you want to go far, you just take them with you.

LESSONS FROM GRANDFATHER

"Sharing the Knowledge" is a story about a grandfather. I just love this one.

As you grow older, well, then you must pick up everyone in the family and spend some special time with them—one person at a time—and tell them things, teach them one thing. Now, you don't want to tell them everything. You don't want them to all be fishermen. You don't want them to all be storytellers, or you don't want to have them all be hunters. You have to spread it all over, so that will make a good community, so that will teach them how community works.

I know a few who were there to witness the actual first drops of water coming through the dam after they broke it down far enough. I know that the dam coming down turned out to be a miracle! They are getting a beach, which they never had before. They've only had big flat rocks, big flat river rocks. No beach, no sand, no clam beds. Now they do have those.

Now they have fish going up the river, now they have crabs moving into the river mouth, and different kinds of clams, littlenecks and also butter clams living in the sand. Those would only roll in after a heavy storm. Now they can go out and dig for them. People are just amazed by this, and so am I.

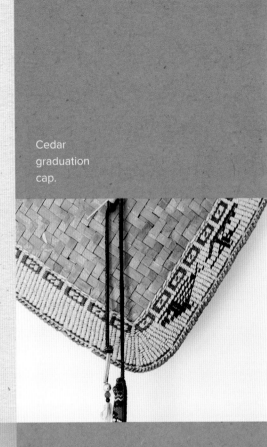

Cedar graduation cap.

Carvings fill Elaine's home.

101

Grandfather was thinking that before he made the trip to the spirit trail, he felt he should share his knowledge. And he had been doing a little bit of it, but the feeling got more intense. And so he thought, I have to get rid of this information I have, and I have to give it to all of my grandchildren, because on the other side of the spirit trail, I can't use all this information I learned. So I should leave it all here for the kids, young ones, and that's what he did.

He walked outside and said, "Yes, I have talked to him, told him, taught him, and oh yes there was a place for girls, too." He then became aware of this little voice, this little body near him. He looked down, and it was his grandson, who was just small. And the little boy was smiling and looking up at him, and he said, "Oh man, ʔuʔ ʔəy' skʷáči ʔaʔ tiə ʔáynəkʷ." He said to him, "Oh, it's a very good day today," and the little boy said, "Ay, yes."

"What are you going to do today?" Grandfather asked him. And this little boy started looking around to see who was there, and he was there all alone with his grandfather. He then realized that his grandfather was talking to him individually. The question was "What are you going to do today?"

The little boy said, "Nothing." He smiled again, looking at Grandfather. And Grandfather said, "Nothing! You can't go from one day to the next without learning something. Look at Grandma over there, she needs the wood piled up. Look over there, you remember your uncle stubbed his toe and broke it. Now he can't go down and fish. You gotta help him, get some food. You have to learn something, to help."

So Grandfather said, "Well, what are you going to do tomorrow?" And the boy said, "Nothing." And Grandfather said, "What? You're not going to do anything? I'll tell you, tomorrow I'm going to come over to get you,

and I'm going to teach you to fish." And the boy asked, "Well who else is coming?" And Grandfather said, "Oh, just you and me."

"Just me, with you?" The little boy turned around to run off. And Grandpa said, "Wait a minute, you need to know when I'm coming. See that mountain right over there?" he asked. "Yeah," said the boy. Grandfather said, "When that sun hits the top of the mountain, I'm going to be rapping on your door, and you better be ready. You better be ready to go with me and bring some lunch, too. Be on time!"

Well, sure enough, as soon as that sun started peeking over that mountain the next day, the little boy got there and away they went down the path. Just then there was some fluttering in the bushes. They both stood still, only moving their eyes. Pretty soon a little black nose poked out, then short little black legs, and a white stripe down the back and up the tail. They let this little Smác'ən' walk across the path and into the bushes on the other side. That's the only thing that moves when there's a Smác'ən' around—that's a skunk. So let her have her way. Let her keep on. "I want you to remember this now. You remember this because it's the little things that will stop you dead in your tracks. It's those little things in life that will do the same thing to you, stop you dead in your tracks."

They went on farther, and out of the bushes jumped a big deer. They all leapt backward in fright. When Grandfather regained his composure, he said, "If I would have had a weapon, the whole village would have eaten for a week." And they both laughed. Then they went on to a great big tall tree at the top of the hill, with a big eagle at the top of the tree. They watched as his head turned all the way around, and Grandfather said, "Wouldn't it be something to be one of those birds? We could see for a looong way."

They took off again and went down to the river. Grandfather had his pack off, and he threw the net out there, and he'd drag it back. Every time he would throw the net out, he would say, "Now you must watch for needs that need to be filled, like your grandmother might have after I'm gone. She'll need someone to get her wood. She'll need something in her life, and you help her. You watch for the needs of all the other people, too."

He took the fish from the net and threw the net out again. "Now, the other thing I want you to do is take your place in this community. You are supposed to take your place. You are supposed to be a leader. I'm leaving you these lessons so you will be a leader. Take care of your people, care for them. Go to them, make sure they're okay." He laid a fish down and threw the net out again. And he said, "I want you to hear something: Never take more than you need, because at some point in your life, there won't be one."

Well, with all these stories going into the boy's head, he began to think, Oh my gosh, I can't learn any more, I'm getting tired. But when Grandfather said, "Son, can I tell you one more lesson?" he thought about it and said, "Oh, yes, I could take one more story."

So with that, Grandfather said, "Do you want me to show you how I can change the course of this river?"

The little boy looked over, and thought, oh, he wanted to change the course of the river. But if he does that— you see it's running wide, it's running deep, and fast— he'll have to create a great big wave! It'll scoop us up, take us down the river, and drown us! Nooo. That won't happen. Grandpa has never hurt me in my whole life, never, not once. And I know he won't do it now.

"Yeah, Grandfather," he said, "I wish you would show me." So with his very large, oh-so-wrinkled, weathered hand, he reached out and cupped it around the boy's shoulder. He drew him in close, and they kneeled down alongside the river, and he said, "Now you watch, you watch what I'm going to do." And so they kneeled down, and Grandfather reached out, and he pulled out a little rock at the edge of the river, and he said, "Now you watch, you watch that." It left a little tiny divet.

The little boy watched and watched . . . and nothing was happening. Grandfather was watching the boy. All at once, the water started coming his direction, and it filled up that hole, and it started coming right for him.

And he said, "See now, I have changed the course of that river. I want you to remember this because at some point in your life, you won't like the way your river is going, and I want you to be able to change it, just a little bit. Doesn't have to be very much, just a little bit, and it will be changed forever."

Elaine with family in regalia.

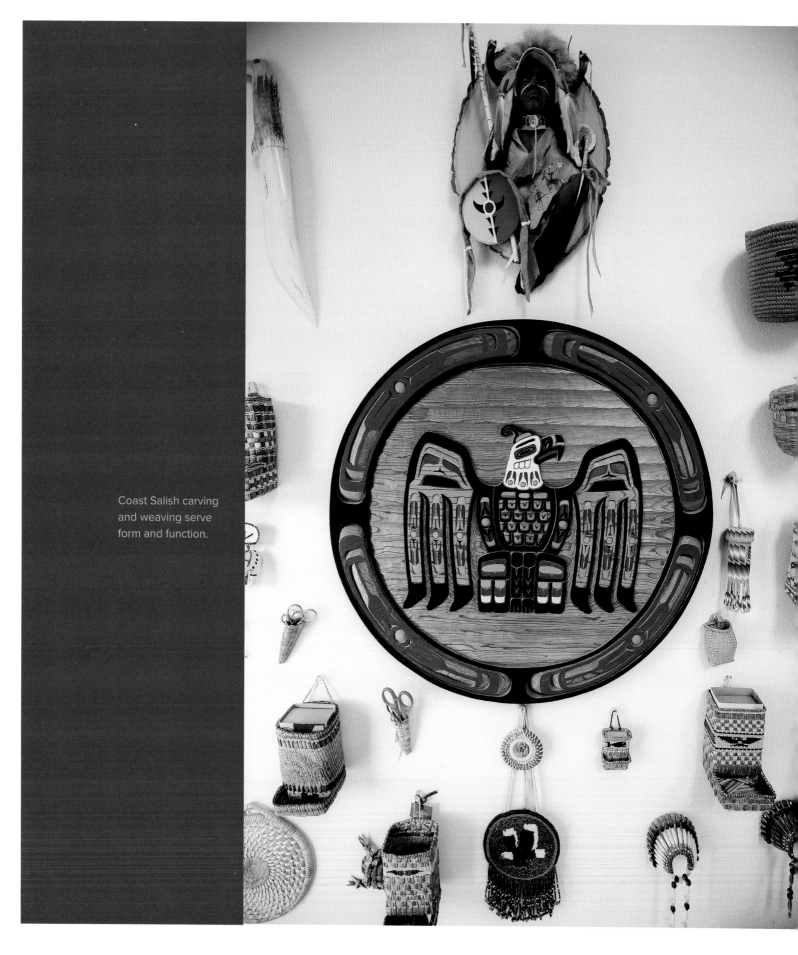

Coast Salish carving
and weaving serve
form and function.

Along with many other traditional pieces, a hand-carved and painted mask hangs in Elaine's home.

It doesn't have to be very much. Just a little bit, and it will be changed forever. And that's the way it is in life. It's the little things. We could all learn from that one. I think that every person, every child, should take the place that God put them here for. To take that responsibility, focus on it, get an education, have good health, and create a good community in which to live. I think that a person's life has a trail that's been trod before, and it might have been by one of our ancestors. That's where our names come from. We have to make the best of what we have within us, and that creates the best feeling.

Even if you do have to assimilate in some ways. I like the washer and dryer, I like this and that. But you can't make me forget that I'm Native. I'm Lummi. I'm Jamestown. And I'll never forget that. When someone says our name or a familiar name, these roads are okay. But there are some roads that just can't be, 'cause that's going to be the ruin of you. That's the value in all of the language. It's not just words. That's the value that you take on yourself, and that spiritual feeling, it's something you can't get over. You can't quit, you just can't quit. That's the knowledge you'll take with you across that spiritual bridge, across, you'll take that, 'cause that's yours.

ARVID CHARLIE

COWICHAN NATION

Coast Salish, what does "Salish" mean to everyone? Whose word is it? My answer to that in court was that they tried to get me to explain Coast Salish, and I said, "I won't go there, that's not our word, that's not our phrase."

That's not my word to explain. They wanted me to explain Coast Salish. I said, "You tell me what you guys mean by it first." I could guess what you guys mean

TRIBAL CANOE JOURNEYS

The canoe journeys began in 1989 with the Paddle to Seattle, a canoe journey undertaken to commemorate the hundredth anniversary of Washington statehood.

That year, fifteen tribal nations and First Nations took part in the paddle. The tribal canoe journeys have grown steadily ever since, with a different Native nation each year acting as host for the pullers and support crews.

The journeys are major logistical undertakings, which the host tribe will prepare for all year. The host tribe will care for thousands of guests arriving from around the Northwest and far beyond, even drawing paddlers from all over the world.

The journey culminates at the host territory with nightly protocol: song, dance, and ceremony, continuing into the wee hours. It is a matter of pride to see how long a canoe family can continue singing. The number of songs a family has is an important form of traditional wealth.

The canoe journeys are alcohol-free and family-friendly gatherings that celebrate the revival of the cultures of the Coast Salish peoples. Guests from non-Indian communities also take part and get better acquainted with the cultures and traditions of their Native neighbors.

Paddling, being on the water, voyaging and visiting—these journeys bring the ancestors into the community's presence. So, while festive, the canoe journeys also have a solemn purpose related to their historic roots. At the Lummi Reservation, the annual Stommish war canoe races began in 1946, when World War I veterans asked people in neighboring tribes and bands to bring their canoes to the reservation for canoe races to honor the returning soldiers from World War II. The tradition continues today, bringing both men and women together to compete in war canoe races from across Coast Salish territory. The canoes themselves are marvels, with some carved the old way, from a single cedar log.

Whether in the canoe journeys or at Stommish, the paddlers' ethic is the same—of pulling together, of honoring the elders and veterans, and reconnecting to the tradition of canoe travel in the homelands and waters of the Coast Salish territories. Physically and spiritually, paddling means going home. — L V M

by it, but I wouldn't guess there on the stand. They recently named the "Salish Sea," and it goes way past us, meaning the Cowichan area, Swinomish area. To us at home, Coast Salish is a little bit smaller world.

From my grandmother Celestine's side, we had relatives from Shelton, and so did Uncle Ernie Rice, on a different branch. He had relatives from there, and his name comes from there. His name comes from Shelton too. For our world now, we're confined by what the governments of the day said. They said, "This is Lummi. You go this far. This is Cowichan. You go this far." They crowded us into reservations. In the past we had communities of families defined not by reservations but by relationships.

PADDLING HOME

It's a long canoe ride down there, and after paddling down to Squaxin, it's no big deal to me. In the past, you were able to camp anywhere. You went so far in one day, depending on the weather and tide. Camped, no problem, usually the whole family. Today, we're expected to stop by the beach, and wait out there, "Ay, can I have permission to come ashore?" No, that wasn't the way it was. I get home, it's my home here. I didn't have to ask permission to come ashore. But today they say we all have to ask permission to come ashore. When I landed at Lummi in 2007, I said, "It's wonderful to be paddling through our waters back in the old days of our family. It's good to be home!"

We started off with the *St. Michael* canoe, and then *St. Michael* broke up, got wrapped up around an anchor rope. So then we paddled the *Mount Prevost*, and then we paddled *Lady Esther*, and from there we drifted around for a little bit.

We went with the *Lydia D*, of Chemainus Bay. We didn't have a canoe, and we paddled *St. Patrick*, Malahat, and we paddled *Geronimo* for a few races. Then I said to the boys, "You know if we're going to keep moving around, we might as well paddle for our own home." So we got on with *Nobby*, five or six of us, then after that we got on with *Quamichan*.

That was twelve years we were winning. We had a long, deep stroke. We tried to stay with that on all of the canoes we paddled, a long reach. Fifty strokes per minute would be super fast for us. Forty-five would be a fast stroke for us, and we were down around forty-one, forty-two strokes. Long reach, deep.

"Let the canoe do the work," I'd have to say. "Let the paddle do the work." Our

opposite Arvid with longtime partner Darlene Gladys Sylvester.

Arvid and family during
Canoe Journey 2018.

paddles were really limber, so they bent, giving you that kicking end. But a person who drifts the paddle, would break our paddles.

I made the paddles and gave a paddle to each paddler. Wayne, one of our paddlers, he had what some would consider the weakest paddle, and he was our strongest paddler and winner. He had such a smooth stroke it never broke. Some of them, we had to build the handles a little more beefy because they'd drift a little bit.

GOOD TIDES

In tribal journeys, if you dare call a canoe a "boat," you're gonna go for a swim — either volunteer or they'll throw you in. We do have a word in the language for Tribal Canoe Journey — it talks about going from one point to some other point by canoe.

This year we're going to Cowichan, East Saanich, Waldron, Lummi. There's no ferry to Waldron Island, so there's no road crew for that trip. We're on our own, we sleep on the beach. In the past, the Waldron community were very good hosts. There used to be an old village there. We all shared it there at Waldron Island. It's about the closest landing point from what is now the Canadian side, so we land at a north beach, good tides come through there. One time we left, going home. It was super rough, but the tide was with us so it was okay. We were towing a canoe back home.

When paddlers switch sides, it's always on the right. There's eight seats, so the guy on right says, "Aight!" You stand up, step forward, and step across, and the other one just slides across, everybody at once. Every canoe, even with thirty people, it's still heavy to carry.

I remember Kitsilano Beach in Vancouver. There were big waves. There was *Rainbow*, *Geronimo*, and *Cowichan Queen*—fast canoes, 1987. And *Lady Seven* and a buckskin crew, the youth. There was no buckskin race. Seven of them came out on their canoe, seven on *Lady Seven*, in 1987.

And the gun went off, and us being fast, we sank real fast, all three of us, bailed out and went again. We left *Lady Seven* way behind, but because they were floating so high they never took on any water and they took the race! Buckskins on *Lady Seven*, with seven paddlers.

Back in the 1920s, you know, there were lots of lady skippers yet. In the twenties, there were pictures of my mother-in-law with a four-person canoe, all the ladies. They're trying to bring them back as the skippers on the six-person canoes. It'd be good to bring them back.

War canoe racing
at Stommish Water Festival,
Lummi Nation.

AMY GEORGE

TSLEIL-WAUTUTH NATION

My dad is from Chief Waut-Salk and Chief Tsleil-Waututh of the Burrard Inlet Indians of the West Vancouver region. And my mom was from Chief Capilano of the North Vancouver area. My parents had an arranged marriage, and they said it would be a good marriage—good teachings from both sides. So they waited till my mom turned sixteen, and she and my dad went into the church, and they got married. So my mom came out and started following her mother. Her mother said, "You can't come with me no more, honey. You're married."

ENVIRONMENTAL PROTECTORS

It is often the grandmothers in Native communities that have led resistance movements to protect the lands and waters of Coast Salish territory. The grandmothers speak for the voiceless, the winged ones, the four-legged ones, and tree people that have long sustained the people.

Tough fighters, witnesses to the suffering of their own elders, the grandmothers and their allies are getting arrested for their people and for their lands and waters. They call themselves protectors, not protestors. Their call of "Warrior Up!" has inspired thousands of supporters.

Native-led, these resistance movements are grounded in traditional knowledge and culture. Social media and communication technology is bringing reach and power to these Native voices in ways that are ever new and still expanding.

As Northwest tribes and bands reclaim self-gov-

ernance and cultural strength, they are increasingly important drivers in environmental protection, not only of their own territories but also the larger Salish Sea—the transboundary waters that connect the US and Canada at the Pacific Northwest edges.

It was the resistance of Coast Salish Native people and their allies that in 2018 stopped the Trans Mountain Pipeline Expansion, which would have tripled the amount of tar sands oil flowing from Alberta, Canada, to the British Columbia coast.

The Canadian Federal Court agreed with tribal governments that sued to block the project because they had not been adequately consulted, and the effects of the project on the animals and waters had not been considered.

Similar reckonings have been successful on the US side of the border, where the Lummi Nation stopped the largest coal port ever proposed in North America,

to defend the Tribal Nation's burial sites and treaty-reserved fishing rights.

Washington tribes also successfully fought all the way to the US Supreme Court to require repair of highway culverts that block access by salmon to their spawning grounds.

The largest ever gathering of Native nations for an environmental cause was Standing Rock, which beginning in the spring of 2016 brought Native people from around the world and their allies to fight the more than 1,000-mile Dakota Access Pipeline.

The movement that grew at Standing Rock did not die there, even after the resistance camp near the Standing Rock Sioux Reservation was forcibly dismantled by police.

Indigenous resistance to fossil fuel projects has continued with support from allies all over the nation and worldwide. — L V M

And she said, "No I am not. I don't want to go with him, I don't know him." And she said they sat down at the table and my grandmother brought the food down, and swish, swish, swosh, everything was gone. The older brother told my dad, "Man, you got a wife, you have to take care of her. Look at her plate. She just has nothing on it and all the food is gone." So my dad would grab things for her. They said, "Oh, please grab the salt," and they all start laughing. "Please pass the butter, please pass the salt," and they laughed.

She was brought up that way, by her mother. We have in my ancestry a John Williams Thomas, from Wales. He was fifteen. When the ship was sailing out, he jumped off. And he just made it ashore right where Lions Gate Bridge is and Chief Capilano's daughter found him, and brought him home, and those two got married, and had my grandmother, so my grandmother was half Welsh, my mom a quarter. Whatever, we got some Welsh blood.

Yes, this is way different now. Back in the day, if a Native woman married a white man, she gave up all her rights as a Native, and then Bill C-31 came in, and they can come back now. We got so many people coming back. Some of them feel hurt because this is the first time they are on their own land and with their own people, so they are hurt, but they don't always show hurt, they show anger. But I am glad they are coming back.

But Chief Capilano had two wives. And there is a family—the Garrisons in Musqueam—but by the end, um, fifty-something years married, he was going to do one of these films and walked up to the house, up to the limousine, and she

started to cry, and I said, "He'll be back in a week or something, Mom." And she said, "I just love that man, so much," she said [she laughs].

After all those years of marriage, that's how they were. And he and his seven brothers, they had built an eleven-paddle canoe called *Burrard Beau*. My uncle Henry George made it, Dad's older brother. And they were winners in that. Their big trip was to Coupeville back then.

PEOPLE OF THE INLET

There were six of us George kids, including my brothers Bob and Leonard. My sisters Rose, Ann, and Irene. And myself—my traditional name is Xaliya. We used to be the performers down in Lummi every year. We would bring our dance

Amy was born into a protector role. She initiated the First Nations call to "Warrior Up" in opposition to proposed oil pipeline projects within her homeland.

Owls are present
throughout Amy's home.

group—our family. And my dad and my brother Bob and Art George, they would play their instruments, drums and rattles, and we would dance. We got a name similar to the Children of the Setting Sun, "Children of Tai Kaya."

During the early 1900s, when there were so many influenza deaths among our people, this man and his wife, he put his wife in the canoe, and he was sick but he paddled up into Indian River [in North Vancouver]. And Indian River flows into this inlet. When they got there, he went ashore and he died, and then she was dying too, but she gave birth to a baby, and the wolves came down, and they were sniffing all around the area, and the mother wolf heard the little baby—a baby boy. And she went over, and she was sniffing the baby and the baby was real hungry, of course, so the wolf laid beside the baby and let him nurse on her. So that baby grew up with them and stayed with them.

My brother Leonard took over leading our group for a while. They are the ones that played at Expo 86 in Vancouver, the World's Fair, with my nephews and my nieces. My brother Leonard has cancer of the throat, so he doesn't do much anymore. Leonard, like our father, was an actor. Leonard was in *Smoke Signals* (1998), *Little Big Man* (1970), and *Chilly Dogs* (2001). Like our father, Chief Dan George, he was also Chief of the Tsleil-Waututh Nation, the Burrard Indian Band, and well known for his wisdom, wit, and work at protecting our First Nations resources and culture.

So, his son Gabe George takes the Children of Tai Kaya here and there, and my dad says, "If you are ever up around Indian Arm, the wolves, they wouldn't touch you because they are going to recognize you as their family. They said they won't harm you. They will recognize you right away."

Tsleil-Waututh, we are Tsleil-Waututh. We are called the People of the Inlet. You see the railway track across the way there? They were going to put it right through here. This is our main reserve, all the way down. There is a park down this way. We have canoe races down there now—Cates Park. They renamed it Whey-Ah-Wichen, Faces the Wind. We lived on both sides of the inlet, from Indian River all the way down, way past Stanley Park. This was all our territory, and we got wiped out by disease and starvation, to just thirteen people.

There was so much death back then. My mom was Christine Jack. Her mother, my grandmother, witnessed it all during her lifetime. She said she remembered they would ring the church bell when someone would die, and they just stopped because there was just so many, so many deaths a day, and they would just do mass graves.

Amy shares her family story over tea.

The early Europeans gave our people smallpox-infested blankets, and we also got measles, mumps, whooping cough—all those European germs we were not used to, they would kill us. An outward murder. They would just, if even three of us gathered, they would have the right to come shoot them all because we weren't allowed to have a meeting.

DAD, CHIEF DAN GEORGE

When my dad, Chief Dan George, became a Hollywood star, it was just so unbelievable. My brother Bob, he played the accordion in a dance band, and this guy saw him and said, "There is this CBC production, *Cariboo Country,* and there's a part for a guy called Born Apart Jon. Would you be willing to try out for the part?" And Bob said, "Sure." So it turned out that Bob could really act, so they did the series. And then one day Bob went into work and they said, "We got some bad news: the actor that plays Old Antoine—the hundred-year-old Indian—he died, so we can't go on." And my brother Bob said, "I can bring you an old Indian." And they said, "Okay, let's try to do that before we wrap it up."

So my brother Bob came home and he said, "Here, Dad, you're going to try out for this. Read this." And he just left the script and went home. So my dad was reading it and reading it. Then he started learning it, and then he went in, and the director and the writer were present, and they read the lines for the other person, and then my dad, and they all started laughing their heads off. And then my dad said, "Am I that bad?" And they said, "No, you're that good!"

Then the writer, Paul St. Pierre, took one of his scripts down to Hollywood and Disney Studios got interested in it because of Dad. They said, "We're going to make a movie, and it's called *A Man Called Smith*," though when they put it out they just called it *Smith!*

And they said, "We're going to buy your script if we can have the 'old Indian.'" So Walt Disney Studios phoned my dad, and my mom was like, "It's for you, Dad," and my dad said, "Hello, oh yeah, I think I have time, sure, be in touch with me. I would be willing, okay, bye." And he goes, "That was Hollywood."

My mom starts screaming and said, "What do they want?" and my dad said, "They're going to do Paul St. Pierre's script, but they want me, with a guarantee that I'll be in it." So he went in his room the night before the airline trip, and my mom said, "What you doing, Dan?" He said, "I'm not going." And it's a real big shame if an Indian says they are going to do this and then they can't. That's a real big no-no for him.

He said, "I'm not going to go. Suppose I can't do it, suppose I freeze." And my mom said, "Dan, you've been practicing for this day all your life. Now you go, and you pack up your clothes, and you get on that plane, and you show them that you have been preparing for this all your life."

That was back in the day when they used to walk outside to get on the airplane. And he wouldn't look back. He just walked to the airplane and went up the stairs. He was too scared. He was nervous. Glenn Ford phoned the house about a year after they made that movie. Rueben, my son, answered and said, "Nope, my grandpap's not here, but I'll tell him you called."

He hung up, and I said, "Who was that?" and he said, "His name was Glenn Ford." Rueben, my son, was just real little. Then Dad got asked to do *Little Big Man* after that. They were just all scrambling because they said, "This is the most natural actor we ever saw." He had no training, nothing. He just went and did it.

He was friends with Dustin Hoffman. When Dad passed away, a cab pulled up, and Dustin came out and stood at the fence of the graveyard, but he didn't go in. He just stood there and probably just said a few prayers, and then he went back in the limousine, and he left. He didn't want to, you know, cause a ruckus. You know how people act? They would probably all run to him, and he didn't want that. You know, what was going on was real dignified, you know, chiefs? And all of his Cree friends came, and they had full regalia on, headdresses.

But Dad met so many interesting people. He was on *Bonanza*. He did *Cancel My Reservation*, *Shadow of the Hawk*, *Josey Wales*, and so many TV shows. He was in *Kung Fu*. He said this young fellow came on, and he was showing David Carradine how to fight, and here it was Bruce Lee.

He was really something. Clint Eastwood loved him. He said, "We go so good together. You want to make another movie with me?" And Dad said, "Oh yeah, I like you too." So they were going to make another movie, but he got stomach cancer, but he never showed it. He had that old way that our mind is stronger than our pain.

TOXIC TAR SANDS

The first I ever saw of the scale of environmental destruction caused by the tar sands projects was eight years ago in our new gym there. They had this meeting with this girl, this young woman activist, Melina Laboucan-Massimo. She brought slides of what's happening in Alberta with the tar sands, and it's so huge. You can see it from space. It used to be all forest and now it's just, well, it's just all sand. It's all torn up, and the tailings ponds are so toxic. I saw them pulling a big black bear out of the tailings pond. The deer, the moose, birds, fish, our people—pull the fish up and under its fin, it has big cancer sores. But they cook it and eat it anyway because they are hungry and they are poor. I walked from sunup to sundown the whole area of the tar sands, and I saw one bird and it was dead on the ground.

Um, people, we went to, we went right in front of the Alberta government. We went right on their steps and made a big gathering there, and we went to the university, and we talked there. Um, all the harm them tar sands are doing. This one woman came up. They felt free to talk when we weren't busy. I was sitting on a chair waiting to go and speak, and she came, and she showed me her arms and her legs, which were all covered with rash.

They said, "Don't bathe your baby in the water more than two minutes, it's so toxic." In some places, you can turn on the water and put a lighter to it, and it will catch on fire. They've never used their tap water for over how many years. Way over ten years, they've never. And you go into the town of Fort McMurray, right from the floor up in the Superstore, right to the ceiling, is bottles of water. They use it to bathe in, to drink, to cook, everything, because their tap water is so toxic.

And that big tank, that big dome across the bay, it might be bigger than that if I remember. Well, it blows pure carbon monoxide, 24-7. After I walked the tar sands, for six months my nose just started bleeding. I came back, and my granddaughter and I were sitting at the mall at Park Royal, and she said, "Tai, your nose is bleeding." And it was, so we had to come back home. I had to get tissue. Just out of the blue, it just started. It sort of has eased up now, but imagine the people that live there, day in and day out. I think it is really pitiful when they say, "Don't bathe your baby more than two minutes in the water, or it will make the baby sick."

So I got involved there, and I have been involved ever since. Yes, Melina came here, with slides, and talked about it, and said what was going to happen: they are going to make pipelines from the tar sands to the head of the inlet. And they are going to dig fifty feet into our inlet and bring in tankers bigger than the tallest Vancouver building. And that's going to ruin the inlet, and the fish life and the birdlife. It is not just *if* there is a spill, but *when* there is a spill. It will kill everything in the area, including us, because we will be breathing in the toxic gasses, and we'd have to move or die here. That's how I see it. There are two choices—to stay and die, or to stop them.

LIKE DAVID AND GOLIATH

Which we've been trying to do. Our Tsleil-Waututh Nation people said, "You're crazy because you are a small reserve, and you're like David fighting Goliath. How are you going to win?" There have been sacrifices through the whole community

opposite Amy shares a story of resistance to oil pipeline development.

to get lawyers, and we are suing the Canadian government for allowing the oil and mining companies to come in.

My son Rueben, he's a Sundance Chief. We've been going down to South Dakota, with Leonard Crow Dog to Sundance, for like twenty years. And he went down to their annual general meeting in Houston, Texas, to Kinder Morgan's annual meeting. Yeah, Richard Kinder. Rueben walked right in there. He showed me a picture from the internet of himself at the meeting. And I thought, "Wonder what he is doing with a big cake?" [he laughs]. But he said, "These are forty-five thousand signatures that I got just over the weekend against Kinder Morgan, against your pipeline and your tar sands."

And he said, "And you promised that everything would be okay, and that you would talk to the people, and we never heard a word from you." Richard slammed the table and said, "Okay, we will come and have a meeting and talk to you." And Rueben goes, "No, you don't have to, you can talk to the Canadian government, because we are suing them for allowing you in, in the first place."

Kinder's face just turned bright red, and Rueben says Kinder was like my other son, who is addicted to drugs. He says, "You look in his eyes, and you see the same thing in Richard Kinder's eyes." He's not at all in touch with his spirit. He's living in a material world, only for material things. He's lost touch with his heart and spirit. They've got the same kind of eyes.

Right across there on Burnaby Mountain, they were starting to clear a path for the pipelines through the mountain, so we went over, and they got the law on their side. While they're multibillionaires—they are worth about $20 billion together, that Kinder Morgan—they said, "You try anything here, we are going to have you arrested."

The founder of Greenpeace was here too. He came here, and we were talking the day before about what's going to happen, and they were going to bring their big ship in too, but the sails were too high to go under the bridge. So Greenpeace had to use their smaller boats.

And farther down, where Kinder Morgan offices are, they put a big sign there. They spray-painted it and hung a sign on it—No Tar Sands, No Pipeline, No Tankers. It was my brother Leonard's wife's mother's funeral, so I said I would go to North Van for about an hour, then I would be back. So I came here, and I saw my family. Then I went back, and they had yellow tape all around the area and around the fence. They had all these guys there, in like SWAT gear and pitch-black with great big guns on she laughs. And so I go—went walking up—and they said, "You can't go in there, ma'am," and I said, "Okay," and I threw what they said aside and walked down to the fence anyway.

We weren't letting anyone in and out for the whole day. And then also on that mountain, there were so many people who showed up to protest that time, and me and the Grand Chief of BC got arrested. They said we are not allowed in the area.

When I passed the yellow ribbon again, Rueben recognized the young brother of a friend of his. His mother is white, and his daddy is Native, and he stayed with us awhile in this house. They are both policemen now. So my son told him, "You take good care of my mother." And he said, "I am going to take good care of her."

He said, "Okay, let's go." And so I went under the ribbon, and the girls started singing the women's warrior song. Oh, I just got so strong. I was kind of nervous to begin with, but I just felt so strong, and then they took us, and they took my name, my address—all my information. And they said, "You know you are under arrest?" And I said, "Yes."

They didn't take me to jail. They just did all the procedure of arresting me, and then they were back and forth on walkie-talkies, on phones and everything. I don't know why they said I had to walk down the whole mountain. It took a long time. I was mud up to my hips.

It was just soggy, really wet. In fact, the police carried me across the worst part. I didn't want them to pack me, to carry me. I thought if I walked through the water, my boots would get clean because I was just sheer mud. And they said, "Nope, we're going to pack you." So, they put the thing down, and it got a little seat, and then I sat on it, and they picked me up, and they packed me across.

Then I walked down, and at the bottom was an ambulance, and they said, "We're going to check your heart," because they said Rueben—my son—told them I had a bad heart. Or I used to, before they opened up my artery with a stent and cleared it.

So then the good news happened. They said, "All those protestors who were arrested, we've pulled back, and we're not going to have her arrested. Not only that, we are letting the people go who were arrested prior to that."

"WARRIOR UP!"

I have been involved a long time now. When we did this thing at a hotel in Vancouver—a big dinner introducing people to who we are and what we are doing—that's when the activist, legal scholar, and carver Jewell James came up from Lummi.

And I was speaking, and I said how the first time I heard about this was at a gym, at a gathering on our reserve. I said, "There comes a time in your life when you put your Game Boy toys down and Warrior Up! Fight for something!" And my nephew, Justin George—I think he was our chief back then—he said, "I'm going to have a T-shirt saying, 'Warrior Up!'"

And he did, and when they did that big march in New York, I saw the signs saying, "Warrior Up!" right across the front of the march. They used it in North Dakota and Standing Rock. My son Rueben was there too, and Jewell went too. They made a totem pole for the people in Manitoba, and then they crossed over to North Dakota, and then they came back that way. In the alleyway, when the news camera was showing that big march in New York, it said my son's words, "You can't put a price on the sacred."

They said at Standing Rock—because Jewell went down with that totem pole, and my son Rueben and people from here went out to show support—they said that when it comes, they will come up here and support us, the people at Standing Rock.

A lot of them, not supporters but the investors—the European investors—backed out first, and the price of oil has gone way down. In court cases, my son Rueben says, we are winning. So if we are like David and Goliath, I guess we are David, and we are winning.

WE ARE PROTECTORS

Usually when I speak at gatherings, we are the ones that started saying that we are protectors, not protestors. 'Cause they said you can arrest a protestor, but why arrest a protector? We are protecting this inlet, and we are protecting the ones that can't talk—the fish, and the bear, and the birds.

And we've been here. Archaeologists say we've been in this area for thirty thousand years, according to our clam beds. And during that time, we had no endangered species. We had no plants that went extinct. The populations were at a level where everyone was fed. We had plenty of food in this area. We each lived according to how good the food supply was and how we could provide for everyone. And the way it is now, I think 50 percent of the animals are going extinct.

Now it is so polluted there is no seaweed out there. I think at the Rhine River in Europe, they've cleaned it up and the water is running clear again because water can clean itself. There is a huge chemical plant just down the road from here. They had a leak once, and my brother was working at a sawmill near there, and about nine of them breathed that chemical in, and their eyes turned yellow, and they just fell over. They took them up to Lions Gate Hospital.

One of several owl collections throughout Amy's home.

124

How long have I known you, Oh Canada? A hundred years? Yes, a hundred years. And many, many years more. And today, when you celebrate your hundred years, Oh Canada, I am sad for all the Indian people throughout the land.

For I have known you when your forests were mine, when they gave me my meat and my clothing. I have known you in your streams and rivers, where your fish flashed and danced in the sun, where the waters said, "Come, come and eat of my abundance." I have known you in the freedom of the winds. And my spirit, like the winds, once roamed your good lands.

But in the long hundred years since the white man came, I have seen my freedom disappear like the salmon going mysteriously out to sea. The white man's strange customs, which I could not understand, pressed down upon me until I could no longer breathe. When I fought to protect my land and my home, I was called a savage. When I neither understood nor welcomed his way of life, I was called lazy. When I tried to rule my people, I was stripped of my authority.

My nation was ignored in your history textbooks. There was little more important in the history of Canada than the buffalo that ranged the plains. I was ridiculed in your plays and motion pictures, and when I drank your firewater, I got drunk—very, very drunk. And I forgot.

Oh Canada, how can I celebrate with you this centenary, this hundred years? Shall I thank you for the reserves that are left to me of my beautiful forests? For the canned fish of my rivers? For the loss of my pride and authority, even among my own people? For the lack of my will to fight back? No! I must forget what's past and gone.

Oh God in heaven! Give me back the courage of the olden chiefs. Let me wrestle with my surroundings. Let me again dominate my environment. Let me humbly accept this new culture and through it rise up and go on.

Oh God! Like the thunderbird of old I shall rise again out of the sea. I shall grab the instruments of the white man's success—his education, his skills—and with these new tools I shall build my race into the proudest segment of your society.

Before I follow the great chiefs who have gone before us, Oh Canada, I shall see these things come to pass. I shall see our young braves and our chiefs sitting in the houses of law and government, ruling and being ruled by the knowledge and freedoms of our great land.

So shall we shatter the barriers of our isolation. So shall the next hundred years be the greatest in the proud history of our tribes and nations.

When my brother's wife walked in and looked at him, she just fainted on the floor because his eyes were yellow. The doctors said, two more breaths at the most and he would have been gone. There is no way to save us if they have a leak like that again, which worries me about earthquakes and stuff, so we want to take that chemical plant out of there too.

There is so much work to do.

I think it's the richest 1 percent: there is 1 percent of our world population that has all the money, and there is not one thing in the world that they don't have a hand in. And they're lost. They are so materialistic that they have lost anything to do with their heart and spirit. Their main object is money, money, money, money, like those two billionaire Texans.

In their lifetime, it would be impossible to spend what they've got now. And they just want more, and more, and more. Now look at all the people getting sick and the animals dying around the tar sands. And they arrest people that protested. I said, "Those are protectors. Arrest the real criminals who are killing all life—the fish, and the bear, and the people, the moose, and the birds. Arrest them. They are the killers. They are the criminals."

We as the red nation, our element is the earth. Not this one little bit of land we're living on, but the whole earth. We've been so hurt by oppression and genocide that we have to get healthy enough to stand up and start protecting the earth ... seriously.

It is amazing, all of the hurricanes, earthquakes, and volcano eruptions. I say, "Well, look at how we have been treating Mother Earth. Mother Earth is a living entity. Do you think she is going to sit there and take all this abuse?" You know, she just has to move a little bit, and it devastates a whole town—a whole country.

One of the main things that we always eat is salmon. We used to have fishermen here, but the water is really polluted.

We used to say, "When the tide goes out, the table is set, with clams, and crabs, and oysters, and fish." Now, there is not only this refinery, but there is a leak, and they said they aren't going to fix it. And the crabs and clams, there are really lots down there right now because we haven't been eating them, they are too sick. We would get sick if we ate them.

In the beginning, I would speak somewhere, and I would talk about our people and how we were wiped out to thirteen people. How we lived here all these years, and we never had endangered species. We could drink out of every creek on the reserve. This water, you could see clear to the bottom, even way out. We would go way out on makeshift rafts, and you could see the crabs walking down below, and we said, "Let's dive down and get it," and we kept trying and trying but it was so deep we couldn't get it. That's how clean it was.

NANCY SHIPPENTOWER

NISQUALLY TRIBE

People tell you different stories, but see, I grew up in the movement for Native American rights. Janet McCloud was my mother, and she started a lot of different organizations and movements. I grew up here at Nisqually. My dad, Donald McCloud, grew up on Frank's Landing. His mother was Angeline Frank, and his stepdad was Willie Frank.

THE FISH WARS

The Fish Wars in Washington State were fought over tribal treaty rights to fish off reservations, in tribal members' usual and accustomed places. These rights were reserved in treaties signed by Native peoples all over western Washington with the federal government. Tribes in these treaties ceded their lands but reserved forever their right to fish, hunt, and gather where they always had.

The treaty rights would be tested over and over in the courts, as non-Indians poured into Indian territories and non-Indian fishers and property owners sought to restrict Native fishing and gathering rights, with the help of Washington State officials.

Game wardens used billy clubs and gunshots to chase off Native fishermen who refused to be pushed off their fishing grounds. Billy Frank Jr., a Nisqually tribal member, was arrested dozens of times defending his people's right to fish at Frank's Landing in Nisqually, near Olympia, Thurston County.

The Fish Wars culminated with fire and explosions on the banks of the Puyallup River in Pierce County, near Tacoma, as game wardens attacked Native fishermen gathered with their allies.

Celebrities such as Marlon Brando brought worldwide attention to the brutality and injustice of the state against its first residents. It took a federal court decision from US judge George Boldt to end the violence, affirming the tribes' right to half the catch. But that did not end the struggle. Tribes have returned to court time and again to force the state to live up to its obligations, not only to respect tribal fishing rights but also to care for the environment on which the salmon depend.

Along the way, a generation of activists who watched their parents getting arrested to defend their fishing rights came of age. Today, they carry on the work to protect the treaties, the salmon, and their Native ways of life. — LVM

My parents' activism rubbed off on all of us as kids, really. My dad, he really didn't like it, because he said it might hurt us in the end. And I think with some of us, it had a lasting effect on us, you know? But not the one he was afraid of. It gave us that strength and that wisdom and purpose.

MY MOTHER

My mother brought spirituality back to us here, especially the use of the sweat lodge. Also the way to say prayers, our way. The way to bury somebody—she brought it back here. She fought for educational rights, for treaty rights, for children's rights. The rights of abused children and victims of domestic violence were big things for her too. She fought for feeding the hungry kids in school, in any school!

She worked on setting up food kitchens, and building housing on tribal reservations. For HUD housing on reservations, the first ten houses built here for the Nisqually Tribe were the result of her work. She also fought for civil rights, the movements led by Martin Luther King Jr. and Malcolm X.

So she did a lot. When we were growing up, she used to get donations, you know, like food and clothes, and she handed those out to all the people in the area. Then she'd get donations for kids, and she would go out and hand those out. And she'd make boxes of things for kids in boarding schools, and she sent them to the boarding schools, all over!

Family photos line the walls of Nancy's home in Nisqually.

Nancy's collection
of sacred objects
and medicines
spans the world.

SHE FOUGHT

She fought for all of those issues, and yet she's not really acknowledged outside
of our family. She was from Tulalip and is buried up there at Tulalip. We got a
beautiful headstone for her. She's buried by Kiya, one of our sacred places. My
mom's Indian name was Yet-si-blu. My Indian name is Wakible.

Isadore Tom was her uncle. And then there was Joe Washington, another
activist. My mother was close with them, so these leaders would come to the
house, all the time, including Kenny Moses and Hank Gobin. She had some real
strong protectors behind her, even Mary Hillaire. We actually went to school with
Mary at Evergreen State College. And then there was Thomas Banyacya from the
Hopi in Arizona. Together they wrote the book about the Hopi prophecies, and

Thomas would interpret them all the time. Then there were the Six Nation chiefs, including Oren Lyons. They were always coming to visit my mother.

These people were always coming and going. My mother was a really well known woman throughout the world. She opened the door for a lot of people and for our fishing rights in the times leading up to the Boldt Decision. Many of our people went to jail for that fishing issue, you know.

OUR PEOPLE USED TO MIGRATE

I fished in Nisqually and Puyallup until they kicked my dad off Nisqually. See, the Boldt Decision, it was harmful in some ways. Our people used to migrate. My dad always fished in Tulalip, too, with my mom. So when the Boldt Decision was being made, you had to pick your area, and my dad was in Nisqually. So they kicked him off the river—he could no longer fish there, even though he grew up on the Nisqually River.

And even today, look at Nisqually in the chum season. Nisqually was the tribe with the biggest chums coming back! I mean, it was a great run! Now, nothing is coming back. They no longer have a chum season. That's always on the news! Who's overharvesting? There's no fish coming back from nowhere. And then there are contaminated fish from the hatcheries, which are killing the natural runs off!

Just like my grandpa would say, "When the fish cease to come, we soon cease to exist." Yeah, we're seeing it now.

And now our kids are flowing right into that movement of rapping and everything else that's on TV, you know? I remember when we were young, we were taught to dance, and bead, and weave baskets, and sew, and everything. Now, nobody does that, or even bake, or cook. See, my daughters will come and say, "Hey, Mom, are you cooking stew tonight?" [she laughs]. And I say, "Yeah, I'll cook the stew" [she laughs again].

So I worry about our future. I'm sitting here listening to my mom saying, "I'm worried about our future." I remember her saying that to people. And we weren't that bad, were we? [she laughs].

GOING TO JAIL

Anyways, a lot of the Puyallups—the ones who went to jail, the ones that they call the renegades—were enrolled in the Puyallup Tribe, except Al Bridges, who was enrolled in Squaxin, I think. I'm not sure. And Uncle Billy Frank was enrolled in Nisqually. He actually was put in jail later than many of the others, and then he

Barbie doll blanketed.

Nancy shares her extensive family archive.

got out later than they did. Yeah, he came in after they were in jail. There were only five in jail at first, then he came in, and then they got out, and he had to stay another week.

But when they went to jail, they went to jail from the courthouse. We were there, as kids. We went to court every time they went to court. My mother would take us there, and we'd watch even though we didn't understand what was going on at first. But when they handcuffed our dad and took him out, then we knew, you know, that he's gone. I actually went to see him.

I was interviewed in 2010 for that documentary film *Back to the River* [from the organization Salmon Defense]. There's a whole bunch of us in it. I told a story about when I went and saw my dad in jail. Um, I really have a hard time telling this story. It's, uh, I think it's one of the most profane emotional things I went through as a child. See? I can't even talk about it.

Me and my sister talked about memories the other day. I think she was four, maybe five, and I was like twelve or thirteen. And when they came up and started beating on everybody and arresting everybody, my grandmother's standing there, holding my sister. And I'm running by crying, 'cause they're dragging my dad up the hill. My dad, and my aunts and uncles, and my mother, and, um, they're dragging them up the hill. And as my grandmother grabs me, I'm trying to get away from her, but the guy takes a picture of us. My grandmother, myself, and my sister, and it lands on the front page of the paper, October 13, 1965.

I remember as a kid, one year we had a beautiful, beautiful Christmas. I mean the presents were just full. I think we got the first Barbies, me and my sister, with the case. That was the only best Christmas I remember. After that it was, meh . . . 'cause they were fighting for their rights then!

Well, then they couldn't even fish. Every time they'd go to fish, they'd go to jail. So it was a constant, constant fight every time they went out there. My dad, they all got their canoes confiscated and everything. My dad's canoe is now sitting in a museum in Tacoma, Washington, and I can't get it. I have to prove it was my dad's, but I have no pictures. But I know that it's his, and it's there, still in jail.

CELEBRITIES

Dick Gregory came over here and went to jail, you know — in Thurston County. And him and Marlon Brando came at the same time 'cause they were all friends. And so he came up and went preaching, and they arrested him. They arrested Dick Gregory for sure, 'cause that was during the civil rights movement. And then they arrested Marlon Brando, but the only thing they did with Marlon Brando was get his autograph!

Jane Fonda was here. She came too. It was called Fort Lawton at the time [now Discovery Park in Seattle], and we did a takeover there. And a whole bunch of us ended up in the stockade. And they released some of us, but Jane Fonda showed up, but what was weird was some of the Indian women leaders got jealous of her. Like, she's taking the limelight from us. 'Cause she did! You know, she just got through making that goofy space movie, whatever it was [*Barbarella*]. So sure, she came out to show support.

So her and my mother got to be good friends. Mom took her out to the prison—McNeil Island—to meet with the inmates out there. And then my mom just took her around and showed her everything. So if you look in *Star* magazine, every once in a while they'll post like a flashback. Well, I used to buy it all the time. I kind of quit buying it, but I bought it one day. There was a picture of my mom and Jane Fonda walking.

So then anyway, Dick Gregory got sentenced to sixty days in jail. And he went on a fast. He said, "I'm not eating nothing until I'm free or you guys recognize the Indigenous people of this land." And so my mother set up a teepee—teepee grounds there—in front of the state capitol right across from the Thurston County jail.

My mother fought for religious freedom for Native Americans in the prison, for them to have a sweat lodge. And she fought hard with the prison, but also with the court, and they had attorneys working with her. So that's how the sweat lodges came to be in the prisons. And then she fought for the Native Americans who didn't want to go to war. Because in the treaties it says that the only way the Indians would have to go to war was if there was war on this land.

136

Nancy shares photos of activist events led by her mother.

This is one of the magazines my mother used to put out. We were young kids with a mimeograph machine, and I had this old typewriter, and we used to have to type on the old stencil. And then my brothers used to have to do the mimeograph, and we put all the papers in line. And my mother was the one that started the Survival of American Indians Association in 1964. She actually started that organization with Don Matheson, my dad, and Aunt Masil. My other sister and my brother have been part of this movement too, our whole family.

NOLAN CHARLES

MUSQUEAM INDIAN BAND

My name is Nolan Charles, I'm from Musqueam. My grandparents on my father's side were Christina Charles and Andrew Charles Sr. When introducing myself through my lineage, I say that I'm the grandson of swəlamθət and θəlθaləma:t. swəlamθət was my grandfather, and θəlθaləma:t is my grandmother.

My father is the late Percy Charles, tᶿətsə́mqən, and my mother is Mary Charles. She was a George. She's a George from Tsleil-Waututh, and my grandparents on my mother's side were Henry and Mary George. I don't know my grandfather's traditional name on my mother's side. And I don't know if my grandmother on my mother's side had a traditional name.

I learned all of my cultural upbringings from my late uncle Andrew Charles, χʷəlsim, and that's what I carry. Am I the gatekeeper? I can't really say that. How do I say it? What I say back home is, I look after properties. The songs were prop-

SELF-GOVERNANCE

Native American tribes and First Nations have a unique legal standing within their countries. They are not interest groups. They are not lobbyists. They are separate, sovereign nations. Their legal status and self-governance were not conferred by the United States or Canada. Rather, it is a reserved aboriginal standing, unaltered by the arrival of non-Natives.

Self-governance has taken new form in the modern era, with tribes and First Nations in some instances creating their own courts and legal systems, school systems, social services, and other governmental roles. Sometimes these services, particularly police and public safety, are carried out in cooperative, formal

agreements with local non-Native governments, for the betterment of the people they each serve.

Self-governance means that tribes and First Nations run their own affairs, elect their own leaders, and determine who may be an enrolled member of their community. Apart from governmental distinctions of enrollment, older laws of family ties and inherited rights of access to lands, waters, and resources unite Coast Salish peoples across the US-Canada border and across tribal affiliations.

These old ways know no boundaries or blood quantum. They unite and sustain the Coast Salish people in an identity rooted in a shared culture. — L V M

opposite Nolan at Silver
Reef Casino and Hotel,
Lummi Nation.

erty of my grandmother, and I look after them for my families. So the songs that we carry in my family, I carry for my grandmother. And they were property of my late uncle Andrew Charles, χʷəlsim, who in turn passed them down to me.

POLITICAL PRISONER NUMBER

I don't carry a traditional name. I had an opportunity to take one a few years back, but back then I didn't feel, for me, that I had earned it. But now that I've been at this game for so long, I think it's about time that I take a traditional name and carry on with what we were taught, basically, in a nutshell. When I go to political gatherings, we have these, I guess in the States they call them "tribal cards," but in Canada we call them "Indian status cards." So I always say that I'm a political prisoner.

When we go to any gathering, and we are asked to step up to the mic, and they ask you to introduce yourself, I never say that my name's Nolan Charles. I say, "I'm political prisoner number fifty-five." The "55" on the card is the Musqueam designation of the Indian Act status card. Every community in Canada has their own. Their numbers start out differently and designate their particular community, and my mother, she's band number seventy-seven. So my mother moved from Burrard, or Tsleil-Waututh, when she was sixteen. I think it's this year that she will have been in Musqueam for seventy years.

Yep. So I come from a community that has 1,300 members. When I started council twenty-four years ago, I think we were at 375, or 400, something like that? So of our 1,300 members, 50 percent of our population is under the age of twenty-five. I got hung up on the factor—the notion that we lost twenty-six members last year. But it was recently pointed out to me in this way: "Okay, maybe you lost twenty-six members last year, but how many did you gain?"

I keep saying, the only ones that're gonna help us is ourselves. We've gotta accept responsibility for things like health and education. The way that the system works in Canada is that the Indian Act perpetuates dependency. You're dependent on the federal government, your nation or your band or your tribe. You're dependent on the federal government for funding, and, in turn, the trickle-down effect says that your memberships "are dependent on the community." It's all, "fix my house, fix my fence, change my lightbulb!" And it's little things like that where it's okay. Well, where does dependency start and where does it stop? So those are some of the things that we're wrestling with back in what is now known as Canada.

Our way to honor our grandfathers and great-grandfathers is to work hard like

they did, because they never took anything for granted. They didn't say, "Well, you owe me." They didn't have that "you owe me" mentality, or they didn't have that "you owe me" attitude. It's not "Is it a right or is it a privilege?" or "Just get out there and hustle." It's like my late aunt Ethel used to say, "Honey, it doesn't matter what you do, you gotta hustle." So prior to this operation for Crohn's that I had, I had three jobs. Now I am back to two jobs, but at some point I want to be back at three jobs.

It was tough growing up on the reserve. I mean, we come from a pretty affluent side of Vancouver. And the irony of it all, there's a major shift going on right now where they look at Vancouver as the gateway to Asia, the gateway to China. Growing up, in high school, I think there were maybe three or four Asian kids in our grade, and I think there were three of us from Musqueam that were in our grade in high school. But now, if you look at the demographics, the non-Asians are the minority and the Asian groups are the majority. So I would [he laughs] hear people I grew up with complain, "I can't afford a house on my own. I can't afford a house in my own neighborhood! It's all being bought up!" And I look at them, and I laugh, and I say to my non-Native friends, the Caucasians, "Well, you know what? Just give yourself 100 to 150 years, and you'll get used to it!" [he laughs]. That's the irony of it all.

I pretty much knew everybody growing up. Everybody, yeah, you knew everybody, heck yeah. Now, with the 1,300 that we have, you look and say, "Whose boy is that? Whose girl is that? Which family do you come from?" And things like that. Like, who are you? Who's that? Yep.

Ha! I always laugh because there was the late elders Ev and Rose Sparrow. Rose Sparrow used to sit at the end of her driveway, and you'd walk by and she'd say, "Who's that!" 'cause she couldn't see too well, and you would explain to her, "Okay, well I'm Nolan."

So then she'd always ask, "Who's your mom?" Because then she could make the connection, "Okay, well you're . . ." I always jokingly said, "I'm Mary's brat, Mary and Percy's brat."

"Okay. Here you go. Keep moving."

THAT CULTURAL DOOR

When I say 375 band members, I knew everybody, heck yeah. We did know everybody, but I never really participated in my culture. We live in a major urban center, and I kind of knew what my culture was about, but I never actively participated until I was eighteen, when my uncle Andrew said, "Well, I'm going to teach your cousin Jim and Delbert Garren's boys how to dance traditionally. Do you want to learn?" Ha! I tell people I didn't open up that cultural door. I kicked it in. It was like holy smokes, so now I'm in there like a dirty shirt—drumming, singing, dancing, the whole enchilada!

The unfortunate thing is, I don't speak fluent, and it's something I need to accept responsibility for and learn how to speak Hul'qumi'num fluently. So that's my next goal in life. I understand a lot of words, and I can string some sentences together, but it's pretty sad, really. That's my next target in life, to learn our language. I took some classes. The University of British Columbia recognizes our language as first- and second-year, but it's taught to non-aboriginal students. So we need to set up regular classes that teach our language. We have drop-ins on Saturdays, but I think we need to do a little more than that. Yep, that's what we, that's what you need—immersion. Use it or lose it.

Nolan is a stand-up comedian by hobby.

Nolan reflects on Canadian and First Nations' relations.

We've probably got a half dozen that are fluent speakers. But the unfortunate thing is that the half dozen don't have enough time. There aren't enough hours in the day to teach everybody.

GOVERNANCE

Well, I keep telling my community, honestly, I'll do it until you get too ornery, get tired of me, and then it's somebody else's turn. But a couple of elections ago, we had a community gathering, and I said to everyone, "Either you can choose not to vote for me, or I can choose not to run, but at the end of the day, I can't choose not to be Musqueam, so I'll be here in some capacity." As an elected official, it is a privilege. Oh boy, is it ever a privilege. Eventually people start to recognize that it's a privilege, not a right, and that this privilege can be taken away at any time.

The general reserve population votes us in. We're transitioning from the Indian Act two-year term to a traditional and formal governance that is a four-year term now. And within this four-year term, we need to have in place our own government system. The federal government says, "We will allow you to move away from the Indian Act government and allow you to develop your own form of governance."

So our little community, we've entered into what they call a "land code," and the land code gives us the opportunity to watch over our own affairs, regarding our own property, without running to Big Brother and saying, We'd like to do this, or, We'd like to do that.

There's some movement in Canada for bands to sign up for land code—develop their own land code and have it ratified by their own membership. And what that does is it gets you out for one-quarter of the Indian Act. So what do we do about the other three-quarters? What do we do to get out from under the Indian Act? The only way to get out is to be self-sustainable—to have the resources so that you can develop the capacity to call your own shots right now. We're not there yet, but we will get there.

I look at mainstream government, and I look at the federal system, and I look at the provincial system, and I say, they're not geared to make the right decision; they're geared to make the popular decision. "How do I make a popular decision that's going to ensure that I get myself re-elected and back in this cushy seat, that makes sure I get my pension, uh, you know, eight to nine years down the road?"

So I have a real problem with—heh heh—any dealing with the feds or the province, but I kind of believe that the attitudes are changing. And I've been privileged to sit at Musqueam's table for . . . this is year twenty-four. After I finish this term, it'll be twenty-eight years of sitting at my council table. I've seen a lot of good, and I've seen a lot of bad.

Relationships with other tribes, they're not bad. It's unfortunate, though. We keep saying, or I keep saying, "There's enough to fill our need, but there's not enough to fill our greed." Because we sit at the mouth of the Fraser River, and we're being challenged by our families from Vancouver Island, who are saying, "We're suing you for a, b, and c," or "We're taking you to court for things like fishing rights or revenue sharing"—some of the things that we are now negotiating with the feds and the province.

They established a treaty process in 1993, and within that six-stage process they ask you to submit your statement of intent. And when you look at the other statements of intent, there's all these overlaps of intent from different communities saying, "That's my territory, that's my territory, that's my territory." Whereas what I said when talking to the province last year was "If I were king for a day . . ."

It's a Nolan Charles opinion, and I've got to state that it's evidently clear [*speaks closer into the mic*]: It's a Nolan Charles opinion. It's not a Musqueam opinion! If I were king for a day, I'd get it all back, because right now, the way the system is geared, you're fighting with your families to say, "That's mine, that's mine, that's mine, that's mine!" Or, as I said to the province last year, "I'd get it all back." And I said, "That's the fight that I look forward to is 'How do we divvy this up?' Not 'That's mine, that's mine.'"

The analogy that I draw is with fishing. When I look at salmon and the salmon stocks, it identifies who we are as aboriginal people in Coast Salish territory. We are part of that stock, or those stocks, and those declining stocks, and that gives us our identity. Not just language gives us our identity. It's the access to salmon, and salmon makes us who we are. So if we start to lose those stocks, then we start to lose our identity.

Who are we without salmon? Period. We aren't who we say we are, and I keep laughing when, every year, we negotiate with the Department of Fisheries and Oceans a percentage of TAC, what they call a total allowable catch. While we're bickering with each other on the riverbank about whose turn it is to throw their net out in the water, the fish are swimming by, but not like they used to, of course. They don't care!

At the end of the day, we have to accept the responsibility for and use our unique status as governments to say we will take the lead in stock rehabilitation. We have always gone to court, and the courts have identified, "Yes, conservation thrives within aboriginal groups." But when do we give back to the resource? Or are we just a resource user?

Have we conditioned ourselves to be like the dominant society and say, "More, more, more, I want more fish!" What are we giving back? What are we doing to give back to the resource? What are we doing to give back to Mother Nature? Or to our Creator? How do we help the Creator? The Creator has helped us through all these years, but now how do we help the Creator?

What kind of message are we sending? Look, you've got declining stocks. Every four years, you have a bounty of salmon called the Adams River Run, but for the other three years, you're struggling just to get fish for your community. So how do we start working together as, we call ourselves, Coast Salish? And how do we, as Coast Salish, develop a plan that gives back, not just takes? That's going to take all the tribes.

THE FORTY-NINTH PARALLEL

In September 2016, I was in Banff, and the tribes of Montana and the bands of Alberta came together to sign a buffalo or a bison treaty. The Buffalo Treaty was initiated by the Indigenous groups on this invisible forty-ninth parallel. Doesn't even really matter, eh? I look at it as we're Coast Salish. I don't recognize that border, the forty-ninth parallel. And same with the Blackfoot people. They say, "Who put this border here?"

Do the bison have some kind of print on the bottom of their foot that they've got to show, like, for their hooves? Ha ha ha, "I'm a Montana bison." No, it doesn't work that way. And same with salmon. They don't know: "Is this American water? Is this Canadian water?" because it's all Salish Sea.

So we're just at the infant stages of doing some exploratory work: does it make sense, and will it work if we adopt the notion or the principles of the Buffalo Treaty and cut-and-paste and develop a salmon treaty? That's what Leroy Little Bear and I were talking about back in March 2017. We got into discussions over lunch back at the Banff Center when I was taking his class, we got to talking about trying to develop something like the Buffalo Treaty. But like I say, "Cut-and-paste and develop a salmon treaty," so we'll take a look at it, and see what will work and what won't work, and I just don't see it not working. Yep.

You can negotiate sovereignty, or you can start to assert sovereignty. So where's the fine line, where's the happy medium?

SALISH IDENTITY

Language—it gives you your identity. It's one. And it's the resources. Like, we look at the Salish Sea. "Is that our soup bowl? The sea urchins, the octopus, the salmon, the halibut—all those things that we draw from the Salish Sea that sustain us?"

Those nourish us, but it's also the things like the cedar tree that we use to build our canoes, to build our longhouses. We fashion mats and hats and clothing from cedar and from bulrushes from the mouths of the rivers. Those also provide us with clothing and mats and things like that. It's all part and parcel. But language is probably the key that gives you your identity, connecting all of these. It will help our little ones prepare themselves for the next battle.

REGROUPING

Because right now, are we regrouping? Have we said, Okay, we've learned the system, the imposed system, that says, "You've got to get an education, and you've got to learn the rules of the game." We've been learning the rules of the game for a long time.

Canada, right now (in 2017), is celebrating its 150th anniversary of the "birth" of Canada. But how many of Canada rode the backs of the 633 First Nations to develop the nation of Canada? Within the history of Canada, what is being taught in the history books that acknowledges the 633 nations in Canada? Very little.

Now they are starting to recognize the Nations in saying, Well, hey, you know what? Within the last twenty years, there's been recognition of and reconciliation over the residential school system. Prime Minister Trudeau was at the Vatican two weeks ago saying to the pope, "The Church needs to apologize, come out and apologize to the Nations, for the imposed residential school system." So I think we're almost at the point where we can acknowledge and get past that and say, "You know what? We got our apology. Now it's time to move on."

Are the people ready to do that, do you think? Well, demographics say that there might be a handful that still hang on to that notion of "they need to apologize," whereas if 15 percent of our population's under the age of twenty-five, how many of the 15 percent of our population even understand what happened? Because it didn't affect them. And now there's 1,300 of us! So our population within that twenty-five-year span has quadrupled. Quadrupled!

So what has remained the same? The attitudes of government. And the unfortunate thing about it is we've had to take them to court every time. We established the treaty process in 1993, and we've realized more through litigation than we have through negotiation. The unfortunate thing about it is that the way that the system is set up, governments don't have to follow their own Supreme Court decisions.

They don't need to implement! "Oh my gosh, hoo, that decision sounds good!" Looks good, but what does it mean? So the attitudes of government . . . I kind of believe that this new liberal government at the federal level is trying to make an effort, because of what they did back in December 2016: they announced a substantial amount of money to go into Indigenous languages.

So they're saying $90 million will be set aside for one year for Indigenous languages. We'll see how far that will go. They're making an effort. Whereas, in the past, I didn't see any governments really making an effort to say, "Well, you know what? We now recognize rights, and title, and things like that." So the fight is just getting warmed up.

RECONCILIATION?

Of this 150-year celebration that Canada is having, how much did we all learn within those 150 years? Well, we have embraced the system and we understand that education is the equalizing factor. Education levels the playing field, and we've learned the dominant society's education. So how do we now educate the dominant society in terms of the ways that aboriginal peoples think? Of being part of the land, and of being a part of the sea, yeah, of being part of the land and sea! (In a nutshell.)

Reconciliation is a buzzword. Who's created these buzzwords "reconciliation" and "accommodation"? Like, what do they really mean? And what's to be "reconciled"? And what is there to "accommodate"? At the end of the day, those are just glorified words to say that we need to sit down and have a wholehearted discussion about what are the next steps. That's just one man's opinion. That's just my personal opinion.

I don't recognize those words, like what do they really mean? What does "reconciliation" really mean? Who's reconciling who? So I just look at those as buzzwords created by the dominant society— "Oo, we're going to reconcile!" Ha!

There's this Native American comedian, Charlie Hill [he laughs]. I saw him on the *Tonight Show* about thirty years ago. It just killed me! Yeah, "So what does 'reconciliation' mean?!" I always adopt the Charlie Hill approach. It just kills me. "Let's rec-on-cile." Ha! Well, at best it's a comedy! What does that mean? All it means is that you need to sit down and have a wholehearted discussion. The governments need to. They can't. I look at mainstream government, and the way they operate is "Let's make the popular decision. Let's not make the right decision.

Nolan showing his Musqueam designation of the Indian Act status card.

Let's make the popular decision that's gonna get me back into this cushy seat, get me re-elected" [he sighs].

So there's a lot of work needs to be done. If you were to ask Jill Average on Main Street in Vancouver, "What do rights and title mean? What does a treaty mean?" her eyes would glaze over and she would kind of look at you. It's what we were talking about earlier: "I don't know!" Heh! Ey? I don't know. I don't know [he laughs].

We've got to create social awareness. Right now there is no social awareness. If you ask anybody on the street, they'd say, "Well, they want it all back." Damn straight. That's what we're expected to achieve by our 633 Nations in Canada. In particular, how many would say 197 in BC, or 203 in BC? Their communities, and in particular my community, would say, "You know what? All of that out there? That belongs to us. We'll get it back."

But what does that mean? What is the foundation, and what do we mean by "We'll get it back"? There are different approaches being developed like this, what they call the ART—Aboriginal Resource Tax.

149

Nolan discusses his role as a representative of the Musqueam Indian Band.

Where urban communities recognize that there's not going to be enough—there *is*, and there *isn't*, enough land to return to the Nations—so in lieu of land, what exists? What moves on the roads? What moves on the rails? What moves through the ports? What moves through the airports? What is our percentage of those things? What is our cut? So there are Nations that are developing that approach to say, "Okay, well, what is our cut?" Do we get two cents on the dollar? Do we get three cents on the dollar? They're looking for innovative ways to say, "Well, in lieu of land, what else is out there?"

This is happening outside the idea of treaty making. This is really just asserting rights to the original homeland. No way my community is going to be offered some lump-sum agreement, and calling it a treaty, the governments will throw it on the table and say, "Here's your treaty!" Ain't happening in my lifetime! Uh-uh. Not gonna happen.

There's so much at stake for my little community. What's at stake is a major urban center. And if we've got three nations that are within that major center, how do we actively work together? We are figuring it out now. It's taking some time, but we'll get there. I say it's about setting the table for the next generation. How do I get the next generation prepared to resume or carry on the fight that our forefathers laid down for us? And I'm thankful to our forefathers, when I say that they didn't sell the farm. They didn't say, "Okay, I'll sign or I'll put my X here, and say we've relinquished any rights or title." Didn't happen. Not going to happen.

HAVING IT ALL

Nothing, nothing has really changed in terms of dealing with the government. What they've said is "Well, you know what, we can't. How do we sell it to the general electorate that we're going to 'give you back your land'? Here's your land back."

So what they devised now is essentially giving the communities or the Nations the right of first refusal. They're gonna sell it anyway. They're gonna sell the land, so what they're saying is "You know what, you guys are now first in line. If we're going to sell these lands, then you've got the right of first refusal."

So isn't that an ideal situation? No, it's not, but it's a solution at least. It's an opportunity at least. "Yeah, okay, we'll buy it back," because we could utilize, or expand, and attract service delivery from our own communities to fight the legal battles. And that's just a detriment in itself because what resources we have, we need to fight for in court. And that detracts from things like service delivery for education and housing and things like that.

If you ask any First Nation in Canada what their waitlist is for postsecondary education, ours is over two hundred. Over two hundred kids waiting to get into postsecondary [colleges and universities]. Over two hundred people that want a home. And everybody wants a single detached home. They have to understand and realize that it might take you twenty to thirty years to get that single detached home. But if we start to provide options like multi-dwelling units, then you get an opportunity to move back home.

And I wouldn't like calling it a reservation, because that's an imposed system. This is your reservation—land set aside and reserved for Indians. Okay, we're going to herd you into this corral and call it a reservation. We only got the right to vote in 1969. That was the first election that aboriginals participated in. We're going to give you your right to vote. Here. You can now vote, in this other system!

And that's what the principles of residential schools were about: *Let's assimilate these heathens. They don't know how to look after themselves* [he laughs]. Oh, well, jeez, I always laugh when they say, "Let's give them something." What is it, 1492, or whenever it was when Columbus showed up, eh? Ha! *Hey, look what I discovered?* Hahaha! Ey? *Look what I found! I found some people! They don't know how to look after themselves. They don't know our ways.* Okay, so what's that, five hundred years of an imposed system?

I guess I'm thankful because colonization started out east—out in eastern Canada, eastern United States—and it took two hundred to three hundred years to get to the West Coast. And by the time it reached the West Coast, the jig was up.

Everyone: "Oh, hey, here are some blankets. You know, you may be a little cold!" Fool me once, shame on you. Fool me twice, shame on me! We ain't accepting smallpox-infested blankets! Ha-ha.

The irony of it all is, if you ask Jill Average on the street, "Do you know what assimilation is?" . . . Do they know what eradication is? Do they know that the whole system was set up in that way? "Let's kill these guys off. We'll give them smallpox-infested blankets and try to kill them off. Because they're an inconvenience. They're in our way! How do we get these little heathens out of the way?"

Your average Canadian doesn't understand our shared history. And when you try to explain to them, they say, "Nu-nu-nu-nu-nu, you Indians want it all!" Well, you know what? We had it all.

ANDY DE LOS ANGÈLES

SNOQUALMIE TRIBE

I'm Chief Andy de los Angeles. I was born in Kirkland, Washington, in 1952. I'm sixty-five. My father was Johnny de los Angeles and was Filipino. My mom was Frances de los Angeles, of the Zackuse clan, and she was Duwamish, Snoqualmie, Lummi, and Irish. She was enrolled in the Snoqualmie Tribe.

My mother and father didn't meet on the reservation. Two of the Zackuse family members had a homestead at the foot of the University of Washington hill. Jim Zackuse—Dr. Jim—had three kids. Jim was my great-grandfather, and he married Amelia, who was half Duwamish and half Snoqualmie. I don't know where they met. It was the 1800s, almost first contact. Their homestead was in Seattle before it was flooded out, when the Army Corps of Engineers flooded Lake Washington. All of a sudden one day, they were notified that they would have to move. The homesteads of George Davis, the Monohon families, and a lot of other families were moved after the treaties, around 1860.

Jimmy Zackuse, or Dr. Jim, was a keeper of our spirit canoes and all of the minor songs or dances. Jim was in old age when they burned his smokehouse down. I think they burned his smokehouse. After that they moved from Seattle to Sammamish. Bill Zackuse, Jim Zackuse's brother, bought land in the town of Sammamish for homesteads. So my great-grandparents, Amelia and Jimmy, lived in Monohon Town. They would survive, then. Dr. Jim was the Indian doctor of the area, and their homestead was on Sammamish land.

My mom and dad are buried at Sunset Hills in Bellevue. George Davis's homestead is on

FEDERAL RECOGNITION

While tribes have been on the lands and waters of Coast Salish territory since time immemorial, not all tribes are federally recognized. Some tribes never signed treaties. Others signed treaties but never sought federal recognition. Recognition does not make a tribe.

In the United States, recognition can be conferred by an act of Congress, or it can be pursued and granted by an administrative procedure initiated by federal agencies and elected officials. Either way, it is a long and often expensive process.

Recognized tribes are able to access federal benefits, such as for health care and housing. They also may put land into trust that may be used only for tribal government purposes. —LVM

Lake Sammamish. I think we still have a claim to that land. We have the Zackuse cemetery, but the land is in King County cemeteries. That's another fight. My grandfather Tom Zackuse was killed hunting bears at the North Fork of the Snoqualmie River. He was young, maybe in his thirties. Nina Kellogg Zackuse was my grandma. She had Elsie, Cora, Mom, Joan, and Jimmy—five kids. I had eight brothers and sisters. I'm the oldest.

BECOMING RECOGNIZED

The Snoqualmie Tribe became recognized by the government in the early 1990s. We're the biggest tribe, related to both Chief Seattle and Chief Pat Kanim (Snoqualmie and Allied Tribes). Duwamish was Chief Seattle, the Suquamish Reservation (because he was buried there). The chiefs were not part of an original council. It was just chiefs of individual tribes. The chiefs' council was not political before either; it was spiritual and of the families' histories. We fought in the Indian Wars of 1855 and 1856 against Chief Leschi. They wanted more land, I think. We were on the side of the Seattle pioneers, though. I know the Denny families and all the pioneer families still.

Our Snoqualmie tribal reservation is trust land near and in Snoqualmie, about a half hour east of Seattle, where the casino and the gas station are. A lot of our land buying was not in trust. The land is now being put into trust, but twenty or thirty years ago, or whatever it's been, we originally bought the land. The Snoqualmie Tribe does not currently have fishing rights. We're still working on that. Our current options are state-run fisheries, like poles—fishing poles, not nets. We are trying to buy a hatchery. The Lummis have a good idea for propagating oysters and clams.

We have two chiefs and the council. It's like other councils. The chiefs don't get a vote; it's an advisory position. I have the most weight because the chairman position is elected by the people to serve for four years. We have a constitutional style of government. I think that's good. There are eight members on the council, and we have one elder on the council. You need to be fifty to be an elder in the Snoqualmie Tribe [he laughs].

The Snoqualmie Tribe still celebrates our ways of the dog salmon and the two sisters—the stories.

The Boldt Decision? Fifty percent of what? Salmon? Fish? I don't know. Yeah, this ain't right! I fished on Lake Washington for sockeyes, kings, and dog salmon. I would get yelled at.

The Muckleshoot and a lot of the Suquamish, we couldn't fish using our nets

Andy shares a staff
he keeps.

Andy at home in Snoqualmie with daughter Sabeqwa.

on Lake Washington, and the Puyallup couldn't fish there too. I would fish south and north of the bridges on Lake Washington. It was big deep fishing. I was a fisheries officer for a while! [he laughs]. We fished also in Elliott Bay and Hood Canal. Oh, man, it was just the ocean, the ocean! And the tides—with the sharks and the jellyfish. After Boldt, we started fishing in the rivers again, too.

I worked on the federal recognition process for Snoqualmie. Federal recognition means that the US legally recognizes a government-to-government relationship with a tribe. At that time, I was overloaded, because I was chairman of a landless tribe (without a reservation) and with no federal anything. Overloaded, oh man.

LEARN AND KNOW THE FAMILIES

A lot was happening in the 1970s, and we are just finding out about the Fish Wars and the Puyallup Fish Wars. It was all part of the civil rights era. During that time, I slowly, slowly started working on federal recognition. The first thing I did was learn about the families. The families are key for learning of the education (or no education), or alcohol, or drugs, or whatever is part of each family's culture. I know the families well.

I was building consensus. I was an expert witness for the King County courts—state and federal. I was a designated "expert witness" because I knew the families. When I first started working toward federal recognition, I was maybe seventeen. I had just graduated. I did this work because I was feeling that our people have some things in common with the Black people and the brown people, and I was angry about our conditions.

Five tribes were trying to get recognized at the same time because of the Boldt Decision and the impact it would have on each tribe's fishing rights. They were the Duwamish, Snoqualmie, Samish, I think Cowlitz, and Stillaguamish. The Duwamish Tribe got left behind in the recognition process, and I don't know why. The Samish Tribe was recognized outside of federal legislative processes but instead in the federal courts. It was a legal decision, not a congressional decision.

The announcement for Snoqualmie's tribal recognition came through the federal register, and the announcement I learned from the assistant secretary of the Bureau of Indian Affairs. When we learned that we were being recognized—wow! We, the Snoqualmie tribal members celebrated—320 of us in the Carnation offices. We had songs, and a lot of people were crying when remembering our ancestors. A lot of the tribal associations—the NCAI [National Congress of American Indians] and ATNI [Affiliated Tribes of Northwest Indians]—had barred us from joining because we're landless and we're urbanized. So it was not always a nice time.

HAVING THE WILL

But we had the will! Wow! Most important is the will. A lot of wives have the will to get tribal recognition. Yeah, I somewhat still see the will in my people. My will has changed because I've had three strokes and three heart attacks, and I don't get out no more. I pray, pray, and pray. I miss Lutie Hillaire. Lutie says, "Pray." Ramona Bennett from Duwamish and Lutie at Lummi, they are the firebrands.

I was there at Fort Lawton during the protests. I was at Wounded Knee in 1973.

Ramona Bennett taught me. She instilled in me the importance of the camera. I was a reporter for the *Tacoma Indian News*. I saw all of that. That day at Fort Lawton, we did a march at the gates, like the civil rights marches. We tried to take over [he laughs]. Some people climbed over the gates.

I marched with Ramona Bennett for civil rights. I was at Gethsemane Cemetery of [the] Puyallup Nation with Ramona and a lot of her people. Because of St. George's Boarding School (in Milton, Washington), the Catholic archdiocese promised to build a trade school. But they forgot us, like what happens to Indians so often. They do have a cemetery of Indians. It was broken down or whatever, but they still have the cemetery. Once, I was riding my motorcycle, and I felt something. I looked around at the forest, at I-5, and I still felt it. It choked me up. They were starting to grade, and I knew the history of that land. There were Indian graves there. And then, I was trying to scream at the one person. I got pictures on black-and-white film, and I kept yelling and tried to stop him. Now, it's the Gethsemane Cemetery.

My last job as an archaeologist was at Semiahmoo Spit and the Tolt River. When the bones of tribal ancestors were found buried at Semiahmoo, I was teaching at the universities and colleges. I was teaching archaeology—how to take care of the ancestors' bones and tribal artifacts. Jewell James was there, and then I think Jewell's cousin worked for King County—G. I. James!

Before that, I was a mental health therapist of the Riverview School District, the Snoqualmie School District, and in private practice for about twenty years. Oh, man, after that, I was working in the newspapers. "Andy has his head cut off!" I was doing so many things at once. Oh, man [he laughs]. Yes, yes, oh, man, I was also working toward the development of the Indian Child Welfare Act. On ICWA, I worked with Charlene Casimir and her mother, Janet Casimir. There were a lot of tragedies, a lot of tragedies.

At the same time I was moving the Snoqualmie Tribe along, I was working weekends and nights. I'm still not retired. I work weekends and some days of the week. I have to. At the offices, I visit and talk about what's going on and look around [he laughs]. Oh, it's trouble.

THE FIGHT CONTINUES

My hopes for the tribes today are to continue on. The Indians are fighting or speaking or whatever is needed, because we are a minority, and minorities have to be listened to. I was on the US Commission on Civil Rights for fifteen years, and they have to listen to us. They have to listen to the families. The fight is not

Andy and daughter Sabeqwa share family photos and stories.

Family photo of baskets, paddle, and fishing technology.

over. It's just beginning. I think there are no salmon, and there is climate change, and there are more pipelines from Canada, and it's more and more stuff! We need the families—it's the families. The families are slowly dying out, and we need to bring the families back together.

It's interesting to see today that a lot of people are still ashamed to be Indian. You know, I wasn't really doing the Indian thing until I was twenty-two, twenty-three years old—my first year of college. Although I knew there was a difference, I struggled with that identity. In fact, how I became a writer was that I was a poet in the late 1960s and early '70s. How I began in the business of writing is that I grew up on a farm, not too far from here. My dad was a Filipino truck farmer back then, and my mother, of course, a Native American. When I started going to college, I took different courses at community college and ended up going to Evergreen State College and got my bachelor's in sociology there. And in so doing, I founded a Tacoma Indian newspaper.

A PRODUCT OF THE AMERICAN INDIAN WOMEN'S SERVICE LEAGUE

One of my first real jobs in the Indian community was in Tacoma working with Ramona Bennett, who was a controversial member of the American Indian Women's Service League at that time because she had some very forward-thinking ideas. She created the first Indian takeover in Washington State, and that takeover was ironically at Gethsemane Cemetery, a cemetery that the Catholic Church was building.

A lot of people recall Fort Lawton as being the only Indian takeover in Washington State, but it really wasn't. A couple of the other Indian takeovers happened after that. One in 1976 was in regard to the Catholic Church and the Puyallup Tribe, and this is a very important issue for tribes across the United States.

Because the churches—the Mormons, the Catholics, the Lutherans (I mean, you just name them)—had cut different deals with different tribes for reservation land. They would either use the land to build a church or, in the situation with the Catholic Church and the Puyallup Nation, they were supposed to create an industrial school, and the land that was given to the church would always be that. They had done the deal perhaps in the late 1860s. The Puyallup Nation wanted the land back because the church was not using it for a school. They were using it as a very posh cemetery. It's one of the nicer cemeteries around that's run by the Catholic Church.

So Ramona Bennett created that demonstration. The Indians won the court case in regard to being prosecuted for trespass. Ironically, Ella Aquino was buried in Gethsemane Cemetery with her husband. And during the time of the trials and during the time of the negotiations between the Puyallup Nation and the Catholic Church, Ella Aquino met several times with the archbishop here in the Pacific Northwest and eventually traveled, and I believe she met with the pope at least four times.

The activism that was spawned out of the American Indian Women's Service League was notable because there was the Gethsemane Cemetery takeover, there was the Puyallup Nation takeover, and some of the fish-ins. The Service League was helping to educate the public because, besides trying to find ways to solve some of the urban populations' problems, activism was their biggest effort.

Regarding the activism, one of the things I learned early on, while being tribal chairman for twelve years and trying to keep a newspaper alive with the help of the Service League, was that you had to do it from a perspective of keeping people together. I mean, anything past that is something for everybody to enjoy, but after that if you don't have the support of the people, you don't really have anything.

I am a product of the American Indian Women's Service League. I am a product of those women who were able to say, "You stop doing this behavior. This is what you really need to be doing. You need to be helping the community." If they weren't there, I probably would have turned out totally different from what I am today. In fact, I know I would. Because of Ella Aquino, Elizabeth Morris, Joan LaFrance, Bobbie Conner—a lot of people who moved back to other tribes. I would be different.

And then, coming back to this point where I was the tribal chairman for my tribe for twelve years, watching Seattle and witnessing the development of Seattle politics and some of the things that the Service League tried to accomplish, the thing I see about this area is that it is like a reservation in so many ways.

You have a group of Alaska Natives, Plains Indians, Indians from the Southwest, the Northeast, all along the West Coast, Canada. You have the biggest amount of population here in the Northwest, and even from my perspective sitting on the Washington State Committee for the US Civil Rights Commission—where we try to track minority concerns and have a good understanding of different populations' problems—the largest amount of Native American population in Washington State is in and near Seattle. The largest amount of problems that the Service League was trying to solve were in this area.

EVOLVING AS A PEOPLE

One of the things we always talk about from tribal perspectives, and one of the things that I have always worried about as a tribal leader, is how we can evolve as a people, and hang on to culture and language, and be able to do all these things with Microsoft, or Boeing, or a government job of some sort.

And it's very difficult, because you have to give up so much. From what I've understood from how the families function in the Seattle area from my previous work—a very intimate and voyeuristic kind of job—is that they give up a lot of their identity to be who they are in an urban situation.

opposite Andy recalls earlier years.

What they hang on to is culture. What they give up is the tribalness—being part of a tribe. I think that what we're probably going to see in the next twenty years or so, is a group of people that are going to be more acculturated than being tribal. Because they will have lost those aspects of religion, language, and that's a trade-off. That's the trade-off that people have to make to be in an urban setting. You know, I'm not saying that in a bad way, and I'm not saying that in a good way. I'm just saying that's the trade-off.

I think agencies such as the Service League have always recognized that trade-off. The Service League always tried to provide situations, activities, and opportunities, to be who they are as Indian people but also to be themselves. And I think in the long run, as we watch tribes evolve, I think that's something that needs to be acknowledged and that tribes need to be a part of. It's important to understand with regard to the evolution of the Seattle Indian community versus a tribal community, versus any community, some of the unique struggles that people go through, that come and go.

There was a time when, as tribal persons, we worried that there were going to be kids that would be half-breeds. There was a time when everybody condemned them through tribal and federal policies. There was a time when we would condemn so-and-so who was from a tribe, and acted like an Indian, and did religious ceremonies with other people, and that's come and gone.

And what we are becoming as a people, in an urban situation, as with the Seattle Indian community, is more acculturated. It's not tribal, but it's more acculturated. And one of the things that people have been recognizing for eighty years, one hundred years—ever since the first urban Indian situation came up on the East Coast—was that those Indians acted more Indian than they did before, or tribally or on a reservation.

We're seeing that, and there was a time when people were angry about what happened with treaty rights. That's changing. You know, the symptoms of the abuses that Native Americans would go through personally have changed. With each succeeding generation they forget about the Indian Wars, or they forget about the time when the federal government tried to abolish treaties and reservations. And I think that's okay, because through organizations like the Service League we can be reminded about some of the good things.

I think in the long run about family, about mothers, about aunts, about the matriarchs who existed 250 years ago or before contact—they remind us about some of those things that are, I think, more important. I think that the years of what I grieve for, as somebody from my age, and my time, about tribe and treaty and that kind of thing, is going to pass. And I think that's okay.

When I defended my right to fish, before the Boldt Decision, tribes had to do this before the Boldt Decision, it was with a gun. I would go out there to fish, and I would have my gun at my side to protect myself and protect my right to do what was guaranteed to me in the treaties. A lot of the organizations back then were crusading.

It was like a big crusade. Not only did we know that wrong things were enacted against us, but we knew we were right, and it was like a crusade. Today, people aren't crusading anymore. We don't have the Joans of Arc. We don't have those anymore. We have people who are very into business. The community is very spread out. People haven't figured out how to get them back together as a community.

The power of the matriarchal system is huge. Without it, you're nobody. Sometimes it was hard for me to tell young Indian women the role—the power—they had. Because as a tribal leader, I recognized that "If you do not have Indian kids, there will be no tribe. If you wish this, then there will be no tribe. If you have Indian kids, there will be a tribe."

And I'm saying this to young Indian women who were unenrollable because they were a part of eight or ten different tribes. They couldn't enroll into any one of them. I'm looking at Indian women who have three-quarters of something else.

To watch the girls carry that, I thought to myself, "Why did I say that? Why did I say that? Because people want to understand the definition of 'Indian'?" It was a very hard thing to put upon them. I saw a lot of depression. I saw a lot of the bursting-the-bubble kind of thing about life—that "I have to be a certain way." And the more I thought about what I said, the more I thought that it was really unfair.

I think that the most important thing is that I can only be sorry or very apologetic about how a lot of people have been raised within the Native community. I don't say that in a bad way, I say that in a good way. I know people have been affected by a lot of traumatic events and they continue to be affected, and I hope that they understand how sincere I am. That I am just one Indian man and that the healing within the community has to come within, and I recognize that from being a tribal leader and all.

JEWELL JAMES

LUMMI NATION

My name is Jewell Praying Wolf James. I was born and raised on the Lummi Reservation. I carry a younger version of Chief Seattle's aboriginal name: Tse-Sealth. Chief Seattle was at the negotiations and signing of the 1855 Treaty of Point Elliott in Mukilteo (Washington Territory), and a leading Native spokesman amongst the tribal delegates. Both my mother's and father's ancestors' lines were there, at the negotiations. I was raised in a reservation family with seven brothers and five sisters. Two of the total were actually older first cousins that my parents adopted. I went to local public schools, attended an Indian boarding school in Oklahoma (up till I almost died from lack of medical attention), returned and finished at

ART AS ACTIVISM

The Coast Salish people of Washington State did not traditionally carve totem poles as we know them, but Jewell James, of the Lummi Nation, has carved many. With the House of Tears Carvers, James has masterfully used totem poles to garner media attention and public engagement in urgent matters of public concern—from combating climate change to freeing the last captive killer whale taken from Puget Sound.

James and his collaborators have carved poles and taken them up and down the West Coast and across the country, stopping at reservations and other communities along the way. The totem poles are a catalyst for community reckoning. They are carved from cedar, among the most vital materials in Coast Salish

culture. The cedar tree embodies strength, endurance, and protection.

Carving a totem pole takes many weeks and hands. Bringing it out as a message to the larger community is in a continuum of Native leadership through art, through story, and through example.

This Native leadership in calling the world to moral account is not new. The shamans and elders of Native tribes and bands have long been a moral touchstone for people of all races. In this tradition, James and his collaborators are modeling how to be Native leaders in a positive, nonviolent movement for change. —LVM

Jewell at the Northwest Indian College Vine Deloria Jr. Symposium with Steven Point (*right*) and Greg Boos (*left*).

Bellingham High School, and then I went to the University of Washington. I completed two separate college degrees: a bachelor of arts in psychology and a bachelor of arts in political science. My long-term goal was law. I did attend my first year of law school (McGeorge School of Law, Sacramento, California) but was asked by the Lummi Nation to defend our fishermen against attacks by the US Internal Revenue Service (which came after the Lummis at the request of a senator known to be anti-Indian).

But getting back to my teen years, I moved out of my parents' house the summer preceding my junior year in high school. My dad gave me the choice between my girlfriend and the family, so of course I went with the girlfriend (my future wife). She and I lived together while in high school, had our first child during our senior year, and got married during our senior year. We lived in an apartment in Bellingham. Outside of school, I was a scuba diver for the Lummi Aquaculture Project and did fishing on the side.

When I was heading off to college (University of Washington), I went home to say goodbye to the family, my younger siblings. We were moving to Seattle, into UW married student housing. My little brother Dale came out of the family house and he had this carving with him. He wanted to show it to me, as his big brother. He was really proud of it, his first effort to make a model totem pole figure.

He was being taught by Lummi master carver Morrie Alexander. The Whatcom Museum in Bellingham had a program funded by a Ford grant. The museum had retained master carvers Al Charles and Morrie Alexander to each train two Native Lummi middle-school youths. The Nolan brothers were being trained by Al Charles, and my brothers Israel James and Dale James were being trained by Morrie Alexander. Only Dale would complete the program and go on to master the art. Dale had been highly recommended as a youth with great artistic potential by art teacher Mrs. Johnson at Shuksan Middle School. So he was really proud to be learning the art of carving totem poles. He had the eye for it. He couldn't read well, but he had the natural artistic talent to learn the traditional arts, two- and three-dimensional.

Right then, with a gleam in his eyes and a captivating smile on his face, I promised to study the art, the stories, and everything on the totem arts I could get my hands on, so I would be there for my little brother. So I started studying Pacific Northwest Coast Indian art in 1972 and did my first carving that year. I was not good at it and needed help. I was lucky that traditional master carver/artist Marvin Oliver was teaching then at the University of Washington. After I took his classes he asked me to be his apprentice, but I was dedicated to studying political science and behavioral psychology and did not want to get sidetracked. So I respectfully declined.

I am now the last carver of the four Lummi artists who started the House of Tears Carvers (incorporated under tribal law, as allowed by federal law), so I've got to keep it alive. I'm the head carver. I do not consider myself a master carver. I usually have several family members or friends help in all my totem pole projects. Whichever nephews and nieces want to help out, they can come over and get involved. They can either clean up, carve, or paint—every little bit helps. So it's been going on since 1972.

Otherwise, I have been a runner for Oren Lyons since 1986. Oren is Faithkeeper of the Turtle Clan of the Onondaga Nation (Seneca), one of the Six Nations of the Haudenosaunee. I've represented him at national and international forums when

A carving awaits painting.

asked to do so. I have participated in drafting the United Nations Declaration on the Rights of Indigenous Peoples (UNDRIP), and for the Lummi I led the Treaty Rights Office (later renamed the Sovereignty and Treaty Protection Office, which was closed down recently). Being involved in tribal leadership for me began back in 1979 and escalated when I joined the Alliance of American Indian Leaders (formed in 1986), which was a group of selected tribal sovereignty elders who gathered together to change the federal Indian policies of the United States.

They planned and organized a lobby campaign to secure a congressional declaration that the United States form of constitutional government was based on the Iroquois vision that led to the formation of the Iroquois Confederacy (see Senate Concurrent Resolution 76, and House Concurrent Resolution 331, which were enacted during the Bicentennial Congresses). Relying on the recent discovery of old federal Indian policy documents and chosen experts, coupled with testimonials of tribal leaders, we proved to Congress that the American form of constitutional government and the idea of popular sovereignty was based on the Iroquois sacred visions. The Founding Fathers were influenced by both the Iroquois Confederacy and the Choctaw Confederacy. In addition, the alliance wanted to prove that we had a government-to-government relationship based on both the written constitution and treaties made. The thing I want you to understand is that the Constitution (which most people don't understand) keeps our Native American sovereignty separate from the United States and the individual states.

We've taken on the IRS for violating our treaty rights and seeking to tax our resource extraction activities. We've battled them based on our sovereignty and treaty rights and our rights to be tribal people as stated in the Constitution. And if you understand the Constitution, then you'll appreciate why our old leaders believed in their treaties, why they believed in their own form of traditional government rather than being forced to "incorporate" under the US per the Indian Reorganization Act of 1932.

Jewell James is recognized as a master carver throughout Coast Salish territory and internationally.

We have to constantly be aware of the need to defend our rights as tribal people, tribal nations. I love to reflect on getting involved in the Indigenous UN debates over the draft "United Nations Declaration on the Rights of Indigenous Peoples." We attended some of the UNDRIP negotiations, and the first thing I heard coming out of the US Department of State were policy positions that were once advocated during the termination era—the early 1950s to the late 1960s, when the US government adopted policies aimed at terminating federal obligations to tribes. I looked around and was like, "Is anybody gonna stand up and object to this BS?" I couldn't take it. I got up, and I challenged the Department of State. "This is wrong! You shouldn't be out advocating these antique, outdated policies! Where are you coming from? Were you advised to do this on behalf of the United States? We are in the era of self-determination and demanding self-government." Our political statement drafted in 2010 in response to those antique termination-era-type policies was accepted by the President of the United States as a legal statement.

See, this is what it's like when we're Native Americans that believe the United States has control of our government. This is colonialism when you believe in the laws that say you can't go visit your cousin when he's right there, just over the border—gotta have a permit, gotta ask the US government, "Can I go see my cousin? He's sick! Or, He's a leader. I need to learn from him." The United Nations Declaration on the Rights of Indigenous Peoples is supposed to be a recovery plan from that type of oppression. There is a lot in the UNDRIP and we cannot go over it all here. But keep it in mind when you hear Native leaders opposing colonialism or neocolonialism.

In each of our legal battles, we're trying to clarify that we have our own traditional, inherent tribal governments. We're a people with rights inherent to us and our nations! It reminds me of the story of the eagle in the chicken coop.

This pioneer farmer is out working his land claim. He's cutting down trees in the forested part of his land. He's turning it into agricultural fields. He's an average Christian farmer. An eaglet falls out of the tree he is chopping down. He sees it fall and thinks, "Poor little eaglet. What am I gonna do with you? I don't know what to do. I don't know how to raise an eagle." So he brings it back to his barn and throws it in the coop with the chickens, thinking the chickens will raise it.

Along comes this wise old Indian. He comes by and sees the eagle in the chicken coop! The eagle is scratching for grubs and worms with the chickens! And the Indian elder says to the farmer, "What are you doing with an eagle in your chicken coop?"

The farmer tells his story and says, "Well, I didn't know what to do. I couldn't raise it. I'm not an eagle. What would you want me to do? It was an eaglet and now it is full grown, and eats side by side with the chickens."

The Native elder says, "I'll take care of it." So the Indian elder takes the eagle out of the chicken coop. He goes out to the nearby hill. He prays to the Great Spirit and he throws the eagle up, saying, "Fly! Go, you are free, my brother!" And it crash-lands down in the valley bottom and simply starts digging for grubs and worms.

And so the elder brings it back to the chicken coop. The next day, he comes back, gets the eagle, and goes off in a second attempt to give him freedom. He told the farmer, "Okay, I'm going to go for a higher hill." He goes atop a higher hill and throws the eagle into the air, saying, "Go! I'm

Close-up of carving patterning.

praying for you! Become an eagle!" Once again the eagle crash-lands into the valley bottom and starts digging for grubs and worms.

In the third-day attempt, the elder climbs a tree on top of the hill and says to the eagle, "Please! Be an eagle!" And he throws it out into the sky. Once again it crash-lands in the valley bottom and starts digging for grubs and worms.

On the fourth day, the elder climbs a cliff—a mountain cliff—and he's looking waaay down below and sees off in the distance the valley bottom. This time it's gonna do it, it is going to fly in freedom. The elder prays to the Great Spirit, "Let this eagle be an eagle!" And he throws it out into the air. The eagle is not trying, like it has a death wish; it is dive-bombing downward and gonna crash.

And just before it hits the ground, it looks up, and there are many other eagles—wild eagles—circling in the high sky, and it swoops up out of the death dive and joins them, and flies away into his inherent freedom. You see, this is what it is like for Native Americans living under the laws of the "farmer" (the United States).

I'm a dreamer. I see things in dreams. I have different types of dreams. I have dreams that tie me to the repatriation of our ancestors' bodies that I can't get away from, and I always get pulled into. Then I have dreams that tie me to the national and international Totem Pole Journeys. And then I have dreams that tie me to fighting the fossil fuel industries in order to protect the rights of people, rivers, and the environment. These dreams, although numerous, are unfolding constantly over time and enfolding together into one life journey. I wish we had more time and space to have a dialogue on how, even today, Native Americans have dreams and visions that guide their lives and spiritual understandings. It is troublesome today for people in general to believe in the spiritual aspects of Creation and time.

We hold both countries responsible and obligated to establish government-to-government relationships with their respective Indigenous Nations and to be open and honest, working in good faith, to enter consultations with the Indigenous Nations for re-establishment of the governmental ethics for co-management of the natural environments and nature within our bioregion.

We declare that we, as Coast Salish Nations, have inherent and inherited rights to co-manage human interaction, interdependency, and dependency upon nature and the respective natural environments of the Salish Sea.

opposite Jewell has gifted totem poles to Native and non-Native communities.

Coast Salish and Allied Tribes

As Indigenous First Nations and peoples we are known collectively today as Coast Salish First Nations. We recognize our combined ancestral homelands in the Pacific Northwest through our relationships and alliances with other First Nations occupying modern western Washington State and southern British Columbia, as well as throughout the Fraser River watershed, Vancouver Island, and all waters that are closer to Vancouver Island than other lands.

As our mutual air, land, and water encompass and compose the watershed system(s) that feed into the Salish Sea, we unite and sign this Peace and Harmony Accord for the Protection of First Nations Peoples and All Creation.

Cosmological Cohesion

We, as Indigenous Nations and peoples of the combined Coast Salish territories, sustain our concepts of the sacred and cosmological cohesion. We continue to create and transmit our philosophy, concepts, principles, and beliefs to the next generations through our songs, dances, ceremonies, sacred regalia, sacred items, sacred concepts and places, our languages, our culture, our traditional practices, our traditional knowledge, including our stories, myths, legends, and folklore, our symbols, and our arts and crafts.

We understand that Creation and all other things and beings preceded our existence, providing human beings with the gifts for our survival. Therefore, we believe in the spiritual aspects of life and Creation and our duty to fit within the Circle of Life.

Binding Spiritual Unity and Rights

From such understandings and teachings of cosmological cohesion, we recognize and respect the rights of nonhuman persons and beings.

Guided by our traditions, culture, ceremonial practices, and traditional knowledge and as taught to us by our ancestors through untold generations, we bind spiritually with the protective rights of all human and nonhuman persons and beings Creation composes. We acknowledge the rights of all beings, human and nonhuman, to experience Creation and life to the fullest capacity.

Time Is a Cherished Commodity

We are taught, through our combined cosmological understandings, that protecting the rights of future generations of children is our responsibility. The honorable aspects of our teachings mandate that we protect all children through time, through future millennia, by our actions in the now, as individuals and as collectives.

All things and all beings are children of Creation with inherent rights. We stand united in protection of Creation and the rights of all children.

Threatened and Endangered Wildlife and Ecologies

We understand that we are not separate from nature but a simple part of Creation, dependent upon all of the rest for our continued existence.

As we are not separate from our homeland, we acknowledge the existence of the Salish Sea and understand its collective watershed systems, its animal, fish, fauna, and flora ecosystems, as composing one natural bioregion, a living entity.

A carving in progress.

We proclaim this collective territory to be a marine sanctuary, and we call for local, national, and international governments to restore natural animal, fish, fauna, and flora populations to a minimum of 50 percent of their historic populations.

Both the United States and Canada

The United States and Canada have endorsed and accepted the principles, duties, and responsibilities and obligations advocated in the United Nations Declaration of the Rights of Indigenous Peoples (enacted by the United Nations, 2007).

We hold both countries responsible and obligated to establish government-to-government relationships with their respective Indigenous Nations and to be open and honest, working in good faith, to enter consultations with the Indigenous Nations for re-establishment of the governmental ethics for co-management of the natural environments and nature within our bioregion.

We declare that we, as Coast Salish Nations, have inherent and inherited rights to co-manage human interaction, interdependency, and dependency upon nature and the respective natural environments of the Salish Sea.

KENNY MOSES SR. FAMILY

TULALIP TRIBAL NATION

JUDY MOSES (*sister*) The Moses family has a lot of branches. We come from the eastern side of Washington, from Wenatchee, from my father's side. And then on my mother's side, she came from some of the Duwamish and grew up around what is now Renton. My father, his father was George Moses, who was Wenatchee. His mother—my father's mother—was Ida Martin, and she was the granddaughter of Chief Sx̌ədiwa (Sonowa) of Snoqualmie.

Our father and mother met in what is now North Bend. North Bend always had festivities, where there would be racing in the streets. The streets at that time were not paved. They were dirt, so they came up and they had horse racing. My father had lived in the area as a farmer and took his horse up there to race, and that's where she saw him. They got to know each other and eventually got married, had eleven kids, starting with my oldest brother Art, who was twenty-two when I was born.

When I was growing up, the valley itself was small. The schools were relatively small. I only had fifty-three graduating from my class and now, of course, they're graduating 360 to 400. So the schools have grown along with the valley. But the kids, we lived near our cousins and relatives, Edward Moses and Albert Moses. Albert lived down by the road. One of the county roads runs through my uncle's property, and so they leased it from my uncle. I believe the documents show they paid one dollar per month, something very small for the use of it.

opposite Kenny Moses Sr.'s regalia.

THE IMPORTANCE OF FAMILY

In Coast Salish lifeways, few things are as important as family. It is within the family that culture is passed on, teachings are instilled, and the joy, and purpose, and center of life are found. While work, or school, military service, or other callings may take a family member far afield for a time, the center is always at and with the family.

Home is where the family is, no matter where that may be. And the youth, as well as the elders, are held to the highest calling: to bring forward the teachings of culture and family to the next generation.

To have culture and knowledge of family—to know who you are and where you come from—is at the center of what it means to be Coast Salish. — LVM

Beadwork by Kenny Moses.

The kids, growing up they had . . . it seemed like for each one on their family there was another kid in our family. So they kind of grew up together. They all used to play together. I tell the kids today, they had baseball, and there was Louie, Morgan, Neil, Al, Bobby, Delbert, Kenny, and Marion—she was a tomboy 'cause she used to go out and play with the boys. They'd get mad at her 'cause she always did better than they did.

When the Second World War started, our family had four brothers and one sister that went in the service. Fortunately, they were all able to come home. Now, Kenny had an accident. They were moving military supplies and there was an explosion, so he was injured from that, went into the hospital, and they sent him back home. When Kenny came back from the service, he was at home with us for a while, then moved to Tulalip to be with Bobby. They were always together.

When he came back, those were the best years for them, playing stick game. Kenny and Bobby were the leaders, and those were just the best years. There was Louie, Morgan, Neil, they used to travel—to Muckleshoot, Sumner, they'd go up to parts around Stillaguamish, then as far over east as Wenatchee. They'd let us know, and we'd follow along with them.

What I really enjoyed doing was watching Kenny and Bobby. Kenny was the leader, so he was the guesser, but he and Bobby would talk, and so he'd look at Bobby, and they'd talk. Bobby would say what he thought, and so they agreed, and Kenny would guess or he'd tell Bobby to go ahead and guess.

They really did good. They were tough to beat. Their main competition, of course, was a white man named Louie Metcalf, and, of course, everybody used to say, "Oh, that's Metcalf." What I really enjoyed watching was when they got the bones, because Kenny was so interesting.

You know, these days you have these baseball players like Ichiro, and they stretch and stretch before the game, you know? Well, Kenny was really interesting, 'cause when he got the bones, he'd hold them up, and he'd cross his arms, toss one this direction and another this direction. He was really fascinating to watch.

Then he met Theresa. You know, they all calmed down. Bobby got married and had some kids, and then Kenny met Theresa and they got married. They all had their families, got out of the stick game, going around and everything. When he was married, he worked in logging, lived in Darrington.

He did enjoy the Indian customs—the carving, beadwork—and eventually served as a healer. He believed in spirituality. It was his, and he was strong in his belief, and he carried it well. People would call on him to come help them, and he did. He traveled from Canada to different parts of Washington. If they called him, someone would be in the hospital, and they would call him. And that's the same with Kenny Jr.

One picture I have here is of a canoe that he carved. Carving, making things, that was his way of relaxing. When he was home with us, he did a lot of beadwork, and he was very talented in that. He'd make the designs. You know, the eagles and everything. He'd draw the picture and put things in squares, the lettering. He was talented. It was something that came easy to him.

Others try to learn, but it was something he didn't have to try hard to learn, he was just naturally talented. Our mother, our parents, they weren't like that. They were farmers, and they worked hard. Our dad worked in the mill and then he had milk cows. It was how they got a little bit of extra money, or they'd sell stock now and then.

I think that he had that talent for people following—wherever he went, they went. With me, it was the stick games. Wherever Bobby and Kenny and the Moses boys went, people went there, whether it was going to be at Sumner, or all the way over in Wenatchee, or at Tampico, up in Yakima. They just had that talent. It takes a special talent.

KENNY MOSES JR. (*son*) When Auntie was talking about Pa getting hurt when he was in the army in an explosion, something that happened, and it got his forearm. That real loud sound? Our house was very, very quiet. Our house was very quiet. We didn't really make much noise.

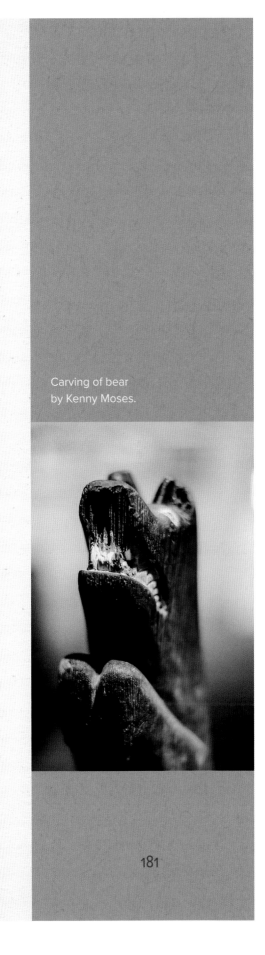

Carving of bear by Kenny Moses.

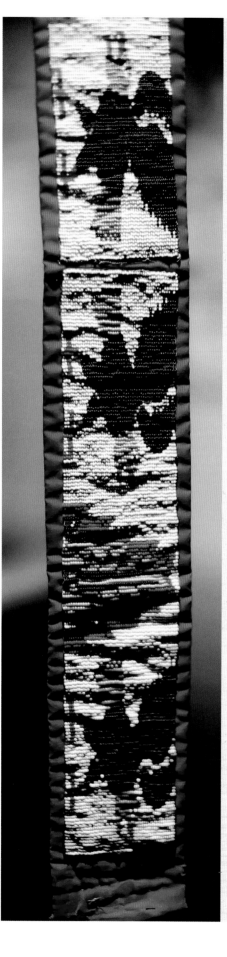

After that accident, that really changed him. He came down to an elder here in Tulalip, and they recommended that he go up to Sauk-Suiattle, to the Suiattle people. That's where they brought out his Sqwedilech, or healer, with the songs and the five different protection powers that he sang in the winter. But with the Sqwedilech ceremonial and spiritual powers, he'd travel all the way from Alaska, all the way down to California. At his funeral, there were people from all over that felt moved to come.

The Suiattle people were his primary teachers, but he had other teachers. The one from here was Nancy Jones. The one from Swinomish was Tommy Bob, and then pretty much all the elders that were still alive in the Suiattle. And the Suiattle—the Indians up there—were free to bring out their songs in the wintertime. They were free to do their gatherings, their potlatches. People would put a lot of work into practicing songs and dances, making gifts, and were really prepared for those gatherings.

In the Suiattle, they had three longhouses. They were used for a week at a time. They had the custom people—the different types of spiritual leaders, singers, and dancers—and my father was a Sqwedilech, and my brother was also a Sqwedilech.

GROWING UP RED-PAINT

KENNY MOSES JR. (son) Our father and grandmother were Red-Paint People, meaning they wore red paint in ceremonies and carried certain gifts and talents not practiced by people who wear black paint, Black-Paint People. So we actually grew up Red-Paint. It was a form of prayer, but we didn't have to really participate all that much, 'cause we were always shielded by our Pa. But we got to learn a lot of the different old teachings. Where we grew up was very isolated, so we were by ourselves with our grandmother and father. So we got to hear a lot of the old teachings, because they were taught at a young age.

When my father joined the smokehouse, where we gather for ceremonies and are taught and practice our spiritual roles, he and Bob Moses traveled a lot, and there were a lot of elders back then that were very worried about our smokehouse way of life continuing. So they had to sit down and listen to a lot of the different elders from Canada, Lummi, Swin. And back then, people were willing to really, really give their Red-Paint teaching. Red-Paint is a little older, and my grandmother and him would talk back and forth. And he actually ended up making new dancers that joined the longhouse.

Much of Kenny's beadwork features eagles and uses red, white, and blue.

above Leatherwork and beadwork by Kenny Moses.

left Beadwork detail.

A painting of canoe voyaging by Kenny Moses.

It takes about two weeks combining Canadian style and the actual Red-Paint way, and they would "make" people. They just brought out their songs through their initiation into the longhouse. We got to hear all of them. For a long time our family was heavily involved in the longhouse. A lot of those days are gone since both of our parents are gone.

My father loved to travel. He went through many, many cars. A lot of the young guys who wanted to learn about smokehouse ways—and spiritual visions and dreams, and how to interpret them—they would want to sit in the front seat with him. You know, in Darrington you're fifty miles from the nearest place, so we traveled lots when we were young. Susan tells about how one year she'd made a calendar for January and February of all the trips we were going on and had gone on, and it was a very full calendar.

SUSAN MOSES (*daughter*) Every month there was one, maybe two days free. It was La Conner one night, Lummi another, Chilliwack, faraway places. Usually, two or three days free in a month, and nobody would talk to him. They would call my mom. She was the calendar lady. She kept that in her head, my mom, Theresa Joseph [her birth name].

KENNY MOSES JR. (*son*): For many, many years, we got acquainted through parades. We did a parade at Everett. We got acquainted with Marvin Stevens, who was from Oklahoma. He sang on a round drum, and so we enjoyed singing. We sang all our lives. The girls are actually better at it than the guys. So for many years my father traveled with the drum during summer and then he traveled with his Sqwedilech. All the new dancers would follow him. Wherever he was going they would go. Growing up it was a lot of fun. It was also a lot of work.

Our family moved down to Tulalip in the 1990s. The three of us kids, we grew up in a logging community—very tight-knit community. We actually felt at home in Darrington. Our home in Darrington burned, had a fire on Christmas Eve. No one was in the house at the time, and the temperature got cold enough a heater turned on and caught a drape on fire.

The fire department, they knew Pa and told the family, "We got out the important stuff." They went in there and got out the Sqwedilech bundle, hunting guns, and some of the fishing poles. The fire department knew. There was actually a few of the tar heels, white men, that held on to the Sqwedilech when they were praying for people. They didn't have any elders, but it could clear their mind still.

Our mother, she went to boarding school on Kuper Island. She made it to the second grade, but got tuberculosis. She was in the hospital for six months. Once she recovered from that, my grandmother wouldn't let her go back to the school. So whenever someone would go to Malahat (where they grew up), they would run into the woods, in case it was like the government or something trying to make them go to school. Our mother grew up very knowledgeable about culture, 'cause she grew up with her mom, my grandmother.

THE RIVER PEOPLE AND SALTWATER PEOPLE

KENNY MOSES JR. (*son*): There are two different teachings that our father really carried. He was teaching us to work as groups, River People and Saltwater People.

The River People, they work by themselves. Just to give you an example, a River Person would cut down a tree, cut it up, and split it by himself. The Saltwater People, which were my mom's people, they work together in groups, and they work real well together. So the men would all get together, and it wouldn't take them very long at all to provide firewood for the winter or for the smokehouse. And the ladies would prepare all the dinners. People would have a good time.

So we grew up in both worlds, both ways. My father was River. My mom was Saltwater. They learned how to work together, so our family can organize a lot of the different gatherings that people put on. We know how to work with all the different families, because of these teachings Pa recognized growing up.

RAMONA MORRIS

LUMMI NATION

My father is Haida, comes from the Edenshaw family, Charles Edenshaw. His parents died when they got the chicken pox and measles—when the white man first came into the Queen Charlotte Islands. His uncle took him in and raised him, so that's where my father came from. Emily, Aunt Emily, was Charlie Edenshaw's oldest daughter, so she remembers all this, and she's the one that told me the history, with her daughter Levina.

They call it Haida Gwaii today. That's the old village. It was tragic. The influenza epidemic happened all over, even in Yakama, because of the US Army. I had a great-granduncle that wouldn't go to a white doctor because he didn't trust him, because the army had brought in blankets infected with measles and chicken pox.

LIVING IN TWO WORLDS AND CULTURAL CONTINUITY

To proudly hold and proclaim both Native American and American identity is a unique stance of Native people. Claiming their roles in two societies, resisting division, and telling the true history of where we all stand: that is their work in this time, and this age, looking forward to the next one hundred years.

The teachings of the First Nations and tribes have new visibility. Natives are leading not only their people but also the larger society in teachings from their elders of living in a shared creation, with all beings. These inherited and inherent rights and cultural knowledge, when shared, are a gift that can protect and enhance the possibilities for all people everywhere to live in harmony and to their full capacity.

In every Coast Salish community there are the culture carriers, people who since earliest age were cultivated to be the bearers of culture for their people. Keepers of genealogy, knowledgeable in the ways of the smokehouse and of the inherent and inherited rights of the families, these culture carriers are the touchstones for the larger community. When a conflict needs to be settled, a confusion needs to be set straight, or guidance is needed, these are the people the community can turn to.

This cultural continuity, this work, falls on the shoulders of a new generation as their elders pass on. They carry on and pass on the teachings of the Coast Salish way of life. It is sacred work, and a journey that never ends. —L V M

These Promises, Governor Stevens made, you heard:

"Americans will take care of you."

It hasn't happened. It hasn't come true, in all phases of history.

This is why as aboriginal people of this land and this country, we're not giving up, we're not going away.

We are going to stay here and we are going to work together.

We are going to become like the great-grandspirit tells us to be—together.

We can solve this problem. We can finish this division.

We have to educate each other. We have to become very knowledgeable as Indian people in how congressional
   people work. We must become understanding.

You and the rest of the country that call themselves American also must be understanding.

We can be understanding together. We don't have to be divided.

Take the time to learn who we really are. We have to teach ourselves the true history of this famous country.

I'm so proud to be Native American, and also American.

(Ramona Morris, in *What About Those Promises?*, 2012)

They didn't know what it was, so they thought it was a rash. They'd go to the river and try to wash it off, some people in so much pain they would kill themselves before the disease took its final toll. There were infected blankets that the army gave out.

That's why the real history isn't written and told. The government says that, oh, they provided blankets, clothes, food, and education. That's their side of the story. Well, when my mother went to Yakama to visit, Great-Grandma Northover didn't even speak English, just Yakama. But she remembered how they were treated, and taken away, and put in schools, forced to wear white clothes, punished. Joe Washington, he told me he remembers when they took him from here and brought him to a residential school. They had a tin can wrapped around his neck. Every time he spoke the Yakama language, he had to spit in the can. That was during Joe Washington's time. So there was a lot of cruel treatment. That's some of the history that was passed on to me.

On my father's side, we're Haida, Yakama, and Colville. My mother's enrolled Yakama. Chief Kamiakin—he's the one that brought the missionaries into Yakama. He gave them protection. That's how most of the Yakamas are Catholics. There was kind of a dispute between the missionaries, when the government allowed missionaries to come in. That's why the Nez Perce are mostly—what are they, Methodist or something?—'cause they got ministers from there. They kind of took over first. There was kind of a struggle between them and the Catholics because they came in to educate us, and to assimilate us, and to teach us their ways. In those days we were called savages and stuff like that, and uneducated, and stupid. We were that in their eyes, because we knew nothing of the white ways. I think each family has different stories and histories of what they were told and what happened with them. This would be just what I have been told.

My grandmother was Suquamish. I have cousins over near Bainbridge Island and Suquamish. My grandmother on my mother's side is buried in Suquamish, but my grandfather is buried in Muckleshoot.

Families in those days used to intermingle and exchange. Then, the chiefs had a lot of wives, so my grandfather had a lot of children. My mother's mother, one of them was from Tulalip. I have a granduncle buried in Tulalip. When they took his Indian name, they gave him the name Solomon. That's why you'll find a lot of English names with really no relatives. They just passed out these names.

There was so much lost in translation. See, land to us wasn't divided, it was

Ramona's cedar hat is a cherished possession.

shared. Then when the non-Indians came, ownership started taking place. You own this, you own that. That's why the government started allotting certain families together: to separate. It was really to separate the families. That's why some have allotment here, some got allotted at Tulalip—especially Lummi was kind of a catchall. That's why we're so . . . you don't really find any full-blood Lummis.

According to Elizabeth Ray's aunts, they were out in the San Juan Islands. The only time they came to the mainland (what they called it) was in the winter. Summertime, they lived out there in the islands. They each had their own spots and everything. I think that's why we have some trust property out there today, because those villages are remnants of it.

This whole blood quantum is a BIA standard. We come from a lot of places. That's why the BIA Constitution was written. Norb James, he was on the council at the time. Norb was related to my mom. He'd make sure I'd have to go to council meetings and listen. The same with Uncle Peter. He was Duwamish, and he was kind of an advocate. I guess they'd call him a "renegade Indian" 'cause he was always fighting against the white rules. He was kind of educated.

Well, anyway, when that discussion came for BIA Constitution, where they had to adopt it, that's why the argument came in where they were trying to put "Lummi" down as a requirement to be "Indian." Mostly all the elders argued against it, because there were hardly any more bloodlines. So that's why they decided "one-quarter blood Indian." That's why it's in the Constitution, "one-quarter blood Indian," so that it didn't leave out the people that were here, and staying here, and allotted here. See, that allotment act messed up Indian Country because that was the government's opportunity to divide and conquer. In my mind, that was the purpose. You got allotments here, allotments there—the Allotment Act.

And then later, if you were married to a Yakama, say, it would go out of trust into fee status. In the 1940s, the BIA started adding those kinds of rules, policies to it. So, it's really sad and confusing. I think my daughter is becoming an expert. For a younger person, she reviewed a lot of these for her master's degree in federal Indian law and understands why things are the way they are today—how we got to where we are.

RAYNETTE (*Ramona's daughter*) There's things that we can do to fight back and change it. Some of these things were done in a different time and a different place. And now tribes are smarter, and stronger, and not poor, and so they can

middle Ramona backstage during the production of the play
What About Those Promises? (2013).

Ramona's cedar hat with copper, abalone, chieftain blue glass, eagle feather, and ermine fur.

Ramona's cedar hat sits next to photos of daughter Raynette's graduation from the University of Tulsa College of Law.

fight these battles, but we all need to come together too. Mom has told me that "you know you can break one stick, but not a bundle." And joining together is what we've struggled to do as tribes. You know, the stories she has, all the tribes in this area all worked together. That's missing. Now, we're in court against each other. We need to solve our own disputes amongst ourselves, not go to the federal government and put it in their courts for them to resolve it for us.

A lot could change. There is an opportunity to change a lot, but one tribe can't do it alone.

RAMONA That's why we need to start educating congressional people. We got to start educating them and teaching them, exchanging with them. They need to understand. When I was involved with legislative issues for the tribe, they were thankful to hear from our side of the story. There was Lucy Covington from Colville, Bob Jim from Yakama, Mel Tonasket from Colville, Joe DeLaCruz from Quinault. We'd all go together. We'd only have three minutes, five minutes or so, to address the assembly, but it was meaningful what we said, because it was our perspective with our values, our understanding. It was educational for them.

In the late 1970s, the IRS started sending notices to the fishermen. I think there were sixteen fishermen that got notices to pay taxes on their fishing income. The chairman of finance (or something with the IRS), he did everything to oppose our bill to reaffirm our treaty fishing rights. He pigeonholed it. He blocked it. He loaded it down with different issues so it wouldn't pass.

Sixteen senators got together and finally moved it out of the committee so it would go on to the House. We had to pass the Senate and pass the House to get to the president's desk. Took us eight years just on the IRS issues related to our fishing rights. We lobbied eight years for that. Raynette was involved in the paperwork. Larry Kinley was chairman. They called me back to help with the lobbying. That was a chore, but we did it.

There were leaders like Jewell James, G. I. James, and activist allies like Dr. Kurt Russo — that's where the Treaty Task Force came into existence, when Sam Cagey was chairman. If it wasn't for the dedication of the community leaders and their allies, we wouldn't have the rights recognized that we do today. And then we piggybacked our self-governance on the tax bill too. That started from the alliance with Oren Lyons. He's an advocate and a fighter, and he's smart.

Ramona delivers the closing to *What About Those Promises?* (2013) in her own words.

Norb James, Jewell's grandfather, is the one that really instilled in me knowing about your history and being Indian. In that old house there, upstairs, he had all kind of books and papers.

He used to hitchhike, 'cause he was Duwamish. He used to hitchhike from here down to Duwamish, in Renton, to help them. When the government disbanded the Duwamish tribe, they just disbanded them. They just did it, scattered them all over. So there was really no village. There was really no group of them living together. They were just scattered amongst the settlers that came into the area. But that's how the settlers took over the country, I guess, at that time.

They put a trail down by the Nooksack River, and Norb had a little house—a little shack down there.

My dad was one of the first to sell fish commercially, because Bornstein Seafood company was just getting started on buying fish. Then Bornstein became friends with my dad, and he built a shed and started buying fish.

I started fishing when I was nine. Not by myself, but Viola Hillaire and I were friends as young girls. We were so small, we had no way to make money. But if we could make a drift, and catch a fish and sell it, we'd get some money. So she'd be on one oar, and I'd be on one oar, and we'd pull together, and set our net out.

In those days people would just, you know, you live that way, and it's not unusual to see kids pulling around. So we used to fish together until I was about twelve or so, before I started getting strong enough to pull the boat by myself and pull the net in.

I caught a beaver once in my net, and I got cussed out. "A beaver, in your boat?" you say. "Well yes, I caught it in my net, and I pulled it in and put it in the fish box, like you're supposed to." And I came home and told my dad that the beaver messed up the boat and messed up the net.

I was more scared of what the beaver was going to do to the net than the beaver chewing a hole in the boat. But he was wrapped up so much in the net, he couldn't chew up anything. My dad got the beaver out and had to cut the net up. Killed the beaver. He was a trapper too. I'd get ten cents for skinning muskrats.

I did all kinds of crazy things. Hunted seals. That's after we got motors. We used to use sailboats. My mom used to make a big sail for Dad out of flour sacks, so he had the biggest sail and a fast boat to race up and down the Nooksack. That was what we did for fun, especially when the wind was really blowing.

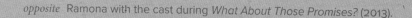

opposite Ramona with the cast during *What About Those Promises?* (2013).

AFTERWORD

Danita Washington

What a journey. What a wonderful journey.

These places that we've traveled, we will continue to travel together, because we still have things to do. I think often about our future and our children. I do hope and pray that you folks' example to the people will continue to be there as a huge prayer that's needed for all of us. Meeting families like yours—some who were able to have or to be parents who could teach—it brings to mind how so many of us didn't have this privilege. The children we see through the work we do, we're still trying to create some wellness amongst our families.

To me, you all are the prime examples of what's thought to be the oldest way, right, and it exists in our time. That's what blows me away. It's like taking a step back in time. I don't know if you feel like this, in the way that you have lived and your families have lived, but that is what it has looked and felt like to me. Being with you all, and how we still exist in this time, amazes me.

And yet we still went to school, and we still got our educations. We can be excluded from and yet immersed, and we can maintain that, and keep ourselves and our children flourishing.

And that is how I will close, for that to be a continued prayer, for yourselves, for your children, and for all of us who need that. Thank you for sharing. You all have a huge legacy to carry on, and we're watching you. Thank you so much.

INDEX